Supernatural
Santa Cruz
Second Edition

Supernatural Santa Cruz

Second Edition

Ghost Legends and Paranormal Phenomenon of Santa Cruz County, California

By Aubrey Graves

Photos and artwork by Aubrey Graves

(Unless otherwise noted)

Copyright © May, 2013: Aubrey Graves
All rights reserved.
Supernatural Santa Cruz – Second Edition
ISBN-10: 148013564X
ISBN-13: 978-1480135642
Graves, Aubrey
Edited by Erika M. Weinert
Photos and artwork by Aubrey Graves (Unless otherwise noted)
Graphic art by Andy Nortik
Cover by Aubrey Graves
Front cover photo by Debi Parola ©

Supernatural Santa Cruz - Second Edition
Aubrey Graves

Dedication

I dedicate this book to all the lost souls of Santa Cruz. May you one day find peace.

Supernatural Santa Cruz - Second Edition
Aubrey Graves

Supernatural Santa Cruz – Second Edition
Aubrey Graves

Special Thanks

Special thanks to Shelley Crowley, LeAndra Johnson, Matt Conceicao, Morgan McGinnis, Brian Carey, Mat Weir, Erika M. Weinert, my uncle (Tommy Graves), my mom and Mr. Jay, Global Paranormal Society, Jeff Dwyer, Kelsey, Garrett, Boccis Cellar, Coffeetopia, The Jury Room, The Asti, Rossi's, Monty's Log Cabin, The Bigfoot Museum, The Bayview Hotel, and last but not least, all of my other interviewees and models.

Supernatural Santa Cruz - Second Edition
Aubrey Graves

Supernatural Santa Cruz - Second Edition
Aubrey Graves

Contents

Introduction 15

Part I: Haunted Sites

Watsonville 23
Mount Madonna   24
Hecker Pass   28
Veteran's Memorial Building   30
The Redman House   32

Aptos 35
Manresa Beach   36
Seabreeze Tavern   37
Bayview Hotel   39

Soquel 45
Soquel Cemetery   46

Capitola 51
The Rispin Mansion   52
The Shadowbrook   56
The Capitola Theater   60

Supernatural Santa Cruz - Second Edition
Aubrey Graves

Santa Cruz **61**

Coffeetopia   62

Dominican Hospital   65

Oakwood Cemetery   67

Rossi's Body Shop and Towing Co.   70

Holy Cross Cemetery   71

Arana Gulch   75

Fuji Restaurant   78

Callahan's Pub   81

Santa Cruz Memorial   84

The Jury Room   87

Water Street Bridge   90

Mission Santa Cruz   91

Bocci's Cellar   98

Evergreen Cemetery   102

Santa Cruz Main Post Office   107

The Vet's Hall   110

The Red Room   112

The Del Mar Theater   115

The Asti   118

Cliff Crest Bed and Breakfast   121

The Santa Cruz Trestle   123

Santa Cruz Beach Boardwalk   125

West Cliff Inn   129

Yogi Temple   134

The Old Wrigley's Building   137

Wilder Ranch   138

Red, White and Blue Beach   142
University of California Santa Cruz   144
Pogonip   151

Davenport 153
Saint Vincent De Paul Catholic Church   154
Waddell Creek   156

Santa Cruz Mountains 159
The Mystery Spot   160
Highway 17   163
Pine Knoll Pet Cemetery   164
Graham Hill Road   166
The San Lorenzo River   168
Santa Cruz Mountain Tunnels   170

Felton 173
Roaring Camp Railroads   174
Felton Covered Bridge   178
Monty's Log Cabin   180
Felton Cemetery   185
Fall Creek   188

Ben Lomond 191
Highlands Park   192
Love Creek   194

Brookdale **197**
Brookdale Lodge   198

Boulder Creek **207**
Boulder Creek Cemetery   208
The Late White Cockade   210

Part II: Confidential Locations

Private Residences **213**
White Lady's   216
The Golden Gate Villa   226
Sunshine Villa   232
The Edwards' House   236
Paradise Park   239
The Walnut Street Incubus   243

Anonymous Businesses **247**
The Old Santa Cruz Hospital   248
The Sister Theaters   250

Part III: Cryptozoology Creatures

Bigfoot in Santa Cruz County   255
The Sea Monster of Monterey Bay   262

Part IV: Surrounding Areas

Pacheco Pass   267

The Monterey Hotel   269

The Winchester Mystery House   273

The Golden Gate Bridge   277

Alcatraz   278

Part V: Miscellaneous and Mystic Enchantment

The Virgin Mary Tree   283

The Sycamore Grove Spider   286

The Ohlone Indians   287

Santa Cruz Psychics   290

Life as a Conduit   298

Alfred Hitchcock   300

Glossary **303**

Sources **309**

Notes **314**

Supernatural Santa Cruz - Second Edition
Aubrey Graves

Supernatural Santa Cruz - Second Edition
Aubrey Graves

Introduction

Originated in 1850, Santa Cruz County is known for its dark historic past and its thin veil to other dimensions. Many spirits are said to dwell in the county, tarrying with a different motive for each one. Famous psychic Sylvia Browne believes Santa Cruz has so much paranormal activity because of the all the moisture in the air, making it more of a comfortable climate for ghosts to reside. No one really knows why each spirit is staying near our plane of existence, yet we can be aware of the reality that they are all around us.

With a spiritual vortex said to inhabit the Santa Cruz Mountains, ghosts throughout, Ohlone curses, Bigfoot and Sea

Monster sightings, I think it's safe to say the county is definitely bounded by the supernatural.

Wall mural on Pacific Avenue and Water Street, Santa Cruz, CA

After extensive research through old articles on microfilm, newspaper clippings, books, the internet, interviewing several locals, and investigating numerous haunted sites, this is what I found in historic Santa Cruz, which translates to *Holy Cross*. Now updated, revised, and expanded, complete with a glossary and maps marked with haunted sites around S.C., I hope you find this book enjoyable and useful.

Happy Haunts!

Supernatural Santa Cruz - Second Edition
Aubrey Graves

Supernatural Santa Cruz - Second Edition
Aubrey Graves

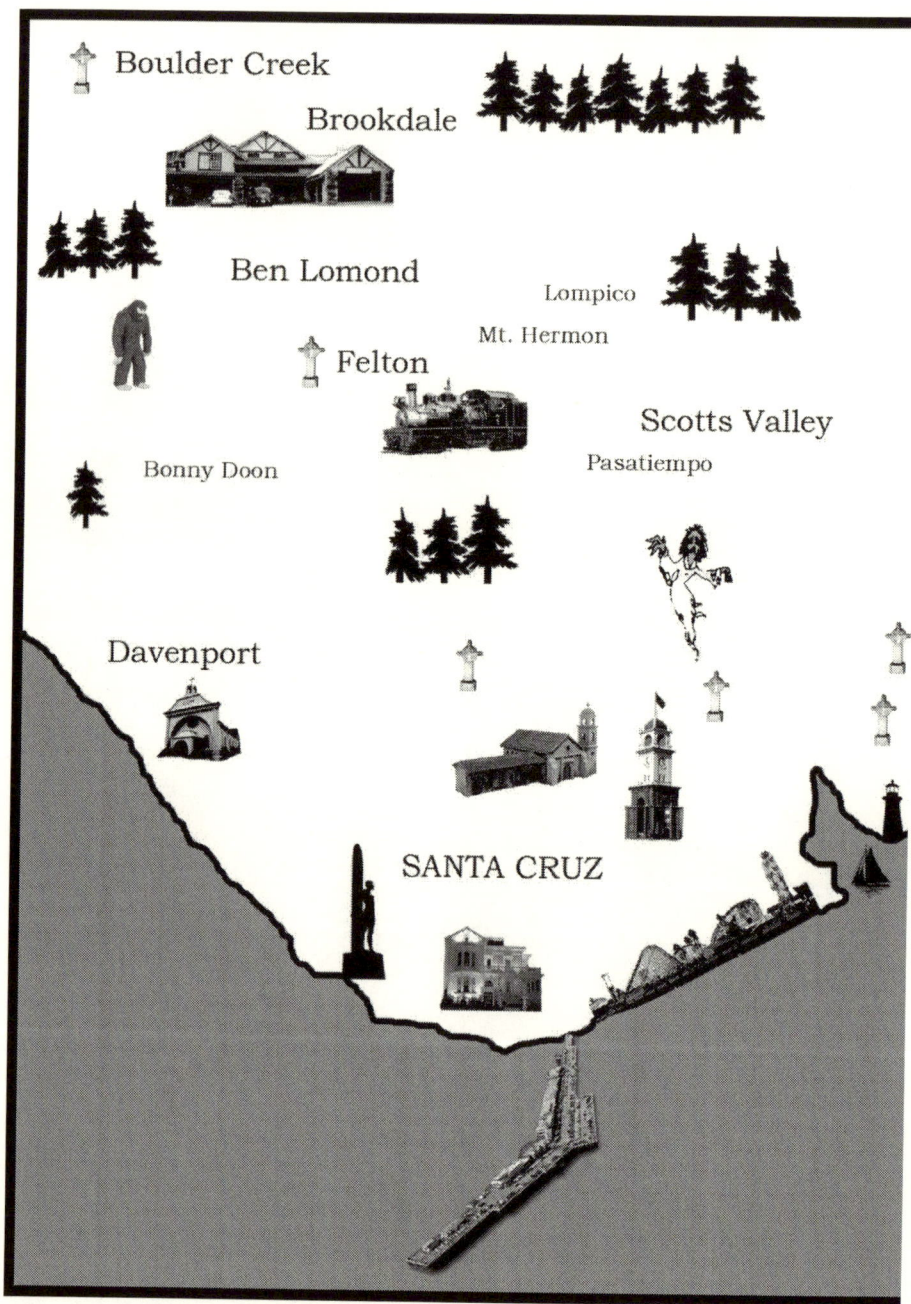

Supernatural Santa Cruz - Second Edition
Aubrey Graves

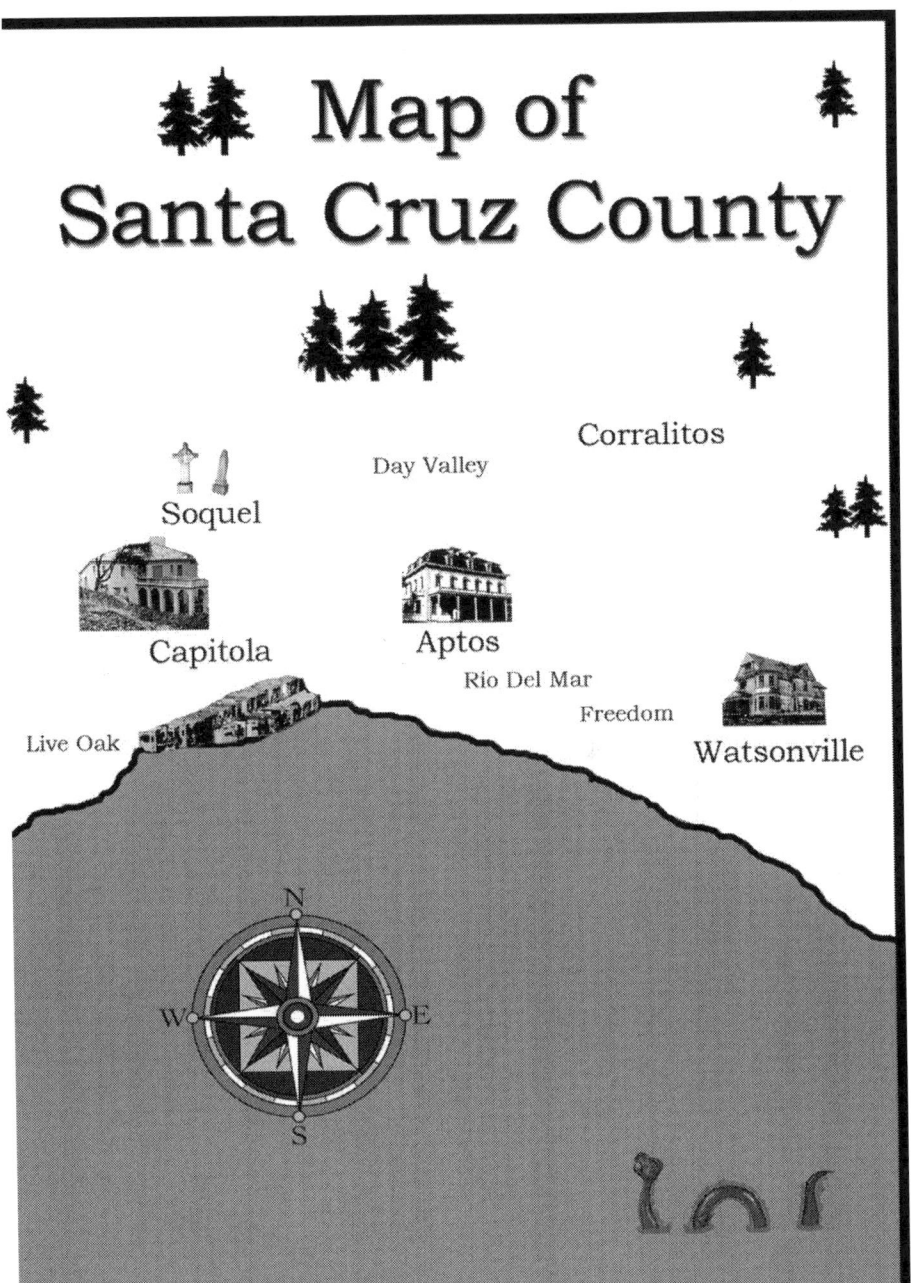

Supernatural Santa Cruz - Second Edition
PART I: Haunted Sites

PART I:
Haunted Sites

Supernatural Santa Cruz - Second Edition
PART I: Haunted Sites

Supernatural Santa Cruz - Second Edition
PART I: Haunted Sites

WATSONVILLE

Downtown Watsonville, CA. Courtesy of Wikimedia Commons

Mount Madonna

Sarah Miller's spirit has been seen around Mount Madonna since her death in 1879. The land was owned by her father, Henry Miller "The Cattle King," one of Gilroy's founders who had bought the land only months before his daughter died. One hot summer day in June, eight-year-old Sarah was riding her 'trusty steed' back to their property when suddenly, her horse tripped, causing Sarah to fall and break her neck. Since then, hundreds of witnesses allege seeing a ghostly apparition on horseback haunt the mountain, and some even claim to see her riding in the back seats of their cars. Legend has it that Sarah is known to get into people's cars, trying to hitch a ride and find her way off the mountain, where she's trapped for eternity.

Miller Mansion Ruins, Watsonville, CA

Sarah is also believed to haunt the Mount Madonna Inn on top of the mountain. Visitors have seen and heard a horse trotting and galloping around the Inn, along with seeing lights turn off and on late at night, when no one was in the building. In recent years, a Park Ranger claimed to have heard a young woman screaming for help from the Mount Madonna Inn. He searched the perimeter of the building and didn't find anyone.

Sarah Miller, late 1870s, courtesy of the Gilroy Museum

Shortly after his death in 1916, Henry Miller's spirit was also felt, sighted, and heard throughout the park.

Henry Miller, early 1900s, public domain

Additional Information:
- Recently, some campers awoke in the morning on Mount Madonna to find horse tracks and small footprints circling their tent.

Location: 7850 Pole Line Road, Watsonville, CA 95076

Hecker Pass

The ghost of a young woman in a red dress has been seen walking along Hecker Pass (Highway 152) for generations by several witnesses. She is known to hitch rides from taxi drivers. They pick her up and then claim that she vanishes suddenly. One cab driver from Watsonville had an experience with the ghost in the red dress, not knowing she was a spirit until the following day. It began one night at around midnight. The taxi driver was near Mount Madonna when a beautiful young woman waved him down and asked for a ride. Contemplating on whether or not to give the lady a ride, (since it was late) he decided to take the woman to her destination. The ghost asked to stop near the bottom of Mount Madonna next to a house that stood alone. He felt the young woman get nervous when they approached her home. The spirit suddenly jumped out of the car and bolted toward the house, not paying her fare for the cab ride.

The next day, the cab driver went to the residence he had seen the young woman run into the night before. An elderly woman opened the door and he began telling her what had transpired the previous evening, describing the young woman in the red dress. The homeowner picked up a framed photo of her two daughters and showed it to the taxi driver. Immediately, the driver recognized the young lady and pointed her out. Shocked, the mother then replied that her daughter had died in a car accident years before as she was heading home. She offered to pay the cab driver, but he insisted that she keep the money.

Hecker Pass, Watsonville, CA

Location: Hecker Pass (Highway 152), Watsonville, CA 95076

Veteran's Memorial Building

The haunted Veteran's Memorial Building of Watsonville was built in 1934 as a memorial for Veterans and as a social center for the town. For years, many individuals have spoken about their supernatural encounters in this aged structure. Several locals have witnessed a little boy on the show stage dressed in outdated clothing, as well as hear the sounds of a ball bouncing. The stage curtains are said to move mysteriously at random times, as if someone is behind them, but there is never anyone nearby.

Veteran's Memorial Building, Watsonville, CA

Visitors have claimed to hear mystifying noises, such as footsteps on the second floor, and the sound of pool balls cracking. There are no pool tables in the Veteran's Memorial Building. Objects are said to mysteriously fall off of shelves in the offices of the Veteran's Memorial Building.

Veteran's Memorial Building, Watsonville, CA

Location: 215 East Beach Street, Watsonville, CA 95076

Supernatural Santa Cruz - Second Edition
PART I: Haunted Sites

The Redman House

The once beautiful, now run-down Queen Anne Victorian called "The Redman House" resides on Lee Road in the middle of a strawberry field in Watsonville, California. This stately home was designed for James Redman by renowned architect William H. Weeks. In the 1930s, the home was sold to the Hirahara Family who owned the home until 1989. The home has been abandoned ever since. In 1998, locals started The Redman House Committee (now known as the Redman-Hirahara Foundation) to try to save and restore the spookish Victorian with donations from the public.

The Redman House, Watsonville, CA

Supernatural Santa Cruz - Second Edition
PART I: Haunted Sites

Amazingly, The Redman is as haunted as it looks. People passing by have seen and heard the spirits that reside in the home. Some people claim to have seen orbs and light anomalies, along with blue and white mists, especially over the shingles of the roof. Legend has it that people were murdered in the house and their angered presence still linger.

The Redman House, Watsonville, CA

Many have heard sounds coming from within the Victorian's walls, and mysteriously from way down the road. Doors have been heard slamming shut loudly on their own, and cool, mystifying breezes have been felt coming from the front door, as if it had just slammed shut. Locals also claim to have heard cries for help from various sexes and ages from within this dreadfully fearsome place.

Additional Information:
- Several years back, ghost hunter, author, and friend Jeff Dwyer, heard two men arguing behind the front door.

- A little boy is said to haunt the home. Numerous locals have heard him scream and cry on various occasions.

The Redman House, Watsonville, CA

Location: Lee Road at Beach Road, Watsonville, CA 95076
www.redmanhouse.com

Supernatural Santa Cruz - Second Edition
PART I: Haunted Sites

APTOS

The Cement Ship, Aptos, CA. Photo by Nicholas Mitchell

Supernatural Santa Cruz - Second Edition
PART I: Haunted Sites

Manresa Beach

This allegedly haunted beach, nestled on the central coast in La Selva near Watsonville, becomes spine chilling as night falls. It is said that in the 1960s a young boy drowned while swimming, and his ghost is said to have inhabited the area ever since. Several visitors have claimed to have experienced uncanny encounters while visiting the beach at night. Some claim to have witnessed splashing in the water, as if someone were drowning, and have also heard the disembodied screams of a child begging for help. Could this just be residual energy left over from the tragic incident? Or could the spirit of this young boy still be roaming the beach endlessly in his doom? I will leave it to you to decide.

Location: Off San Andreas Road, La Selva, CA 95076

Supernatural Santa Cruz - Second Edition
PART I: Haunted Sites

Seabreeze Tavern

A building overlooking Monterey Bay in the Rio Del Mar flats, known as "the local haunted house," is said to be haunted by the bar's first owner, whose untimely death occurred within this structure. Georgia May Derber was born May 1, 1943 in Columbus, Georgia. She moved to Santa Cruz County in 1970 and purchased the 1927 Spanish-Style building and opened it as the Seabreeze Tavern in 1970.

The Seabreeze Tavern, Aptos, CA

The Natalie Wood look-alike ran the bar until 1988, when she became a recluse, rarely leaving her apartment above the tavern for 16 years. On June 8th, 2004, Georgia's mummified body was found on her kitchen floor from complications due to cancer. Because of her reclusive behavior, her body was unnoticed for quite some time until a Sheriff's deputy just happened to stop by to check up on her one day.

The Seabreeze Tavern, Aptos, CA

In 2007, the Tavern was refurbished and reopened, keeping Georgia in mind. It is claimed that she never left the structure, her ghost still lingering in the vicinity. Fortunately, Georgia is said to be happy with the updated establishment.

Location: 101 Esplanade, Aptos, CA 95003

Bayview Hotel

The gallant Bayview Hotel was built in 1878 and still stands on Soquel Drive in Aptos. This amazing Victorian structure has been visited by many famous, prominent people, including Lillian Russell, and King Kalakaua of Hawaii. The bed and breakfast has had several different owners over the years and is operated as a hotel, bar, and restaurant. It is alleged that in the 1860s, hundreds of people who died of disease were buried in one single grave located behind the Bayview.

The Bayview Hotel, Aptos, CA

Supernatural Santa Cruz - Second Edition
PART I: Haunted Sites

For more than a century, spirits have roamed this hotel, making their presence known by creating an abundance of disturbances with their enigmatic energies. It's a well-known fact that customers will up and leave in the middle of the night because they are scared out of their wits.

The Bayview Hotel, circa 1900, Aptos, CA. Courtesy of the Bayview Hotel

I spoke with Christina, the Bayview's current owner since 2002, who affirms that the Hotel is indeed haunted. It would take her all day to explain all of her encounters with the ghosts who reside there. Christina's first experience was on her very first night in the hotel. She felt a cold gust of wind, and then smelled the scent of roses. Christina turned to where she felt the breeze in the hallway and saw the apparition of a woman standing on the other side of the mirror. Christina's bed would also shake violently right before she would go to sleep . . . every night for six months.

Christina and her daughters live on the third story of the hotel. They believe that visitors from the past must have passed away on the top floor, possibly the past owners who allegedly died there long ago. I asked Christina where the most paranormal occurrences happen and she verified that it is on the entire second level. The bar at the Bayview is known to have lots of paranormal activity as well.

Bayview Hotel, Aptos, CA

Supernatural Santa Cruz - Second Edition
PART I: Haunted Sites

A couple of months before I visited the hotel, Christina's daughter had taken a photo of her refection in the hall mirror. Upon reviewing the photo, she noticed a hand coming from the opposite side of the mirror pushing out from the glass. All staff members, as well as the owner and her two daughters have had numerous accounts of paranormal experiences. Ghosts residing at the hotel are known to turn computers and televisions on and off, and change channels right in front of viewers. From stirring apparitions and dark shadows to faces, orbs, moving objects, disembodied voices, eerie sounds, and its very own graveyard, this haunted hotel really has it all.

Bayview Hotel, Aptos, CA

Supernatural Santa Cruz - Second Edition
PART I: Haunted Sites

Additional Information:
- Many have heard footsteps and singing in the halls.

- In 2000, a guest saw ghosts of what looked to be a mother and child in the bathroom.

- The ghost of a little boy is said to knock on the doors, and has been seen looking out a window and suddenly vanishing.

- Previous owners claimed to also have multiple paranormal experiences, including:
  - Being "waved at" by a ghost.
  - A large framed picture being tilted by an unseen entity in the same direction every day.
  - Receiving a helping hand from the spirits who manually started up the large heavy pendulum clock when it stopped. (Santa Cruz Sentinel, 2000.)

Location: 8041 Soquel Drive, Aptos, CA 95003

(831) 688-8654

www.bayviewhotel.com

Supernatural Santa Cruz - Second Edition
PART I: Haunted Sites

Supernatural Santa Cruz - Second Edition
PART I: Haunted Sites

SOQUEL

Soquel Village, CA, public domain photo by unknown

Soquel Cemetery

Old Soquel Cemetery, also known as the Eternal Home Cemetery, is located in the rolling hills in the city of Soquel, California. Since my husband Sean's and my paranormal experiences one sunny Sunday afternoon, I believe the property is very active with ghostly phenomenon, even in broad daylight. As we arrived at the cemetery, we walked around to see if I felt drawn to any particular gravesite. Within ten minutes, I was drawn to a grave that I felt had energy. I got out my Ghost Meter and it showed high EMF readings in front of the gravesite, verifying my perception. Making sure that the Ghost Meter wasn't picking up any surrounding electrical poles, I noticed there were none on the property along Soquel Creek.

Supernatural Santa Cruz - Second Edition
PART I: Haunted Sites

Soquel Cemetery, Soquel, CA

I first tried doing an EVP session, but was unable to get anything substantial due to the noise on the road. I began using the flashlight method to communicate with the spirit of an 18-year-old girl whose name I will keep anonymous. While speaking with her for about thirty minutes, I found out that she knew she was dead and how she died, that she was aware of a better place for her to go, and she was ready to cross over, but needed assistance. I had never helped cross a spirit over on my own before, but had learned how to within the last year and figured I might as well try. After calling on her and my spirit guides, as well as her ancestors to help guide her to the light, I meditated and concentrated on helping this girl cross over for about ten minutes. Almost immediately I felt relief.

"Did you find the light?" I asked.

The flashlight flickered in affirmation.

"Is this a spirit guide saying, 'Thank you?'"

The light turned on once more.

I began to feel very nauseous as I walked away from the young woman's gravesite. I turned on my Ghost Meter again and it read extremely high EMF all around me. I wondered if I really just helped an earth-bound spirit cross over, and if so, maybe others were beginning to follow me for assistance.

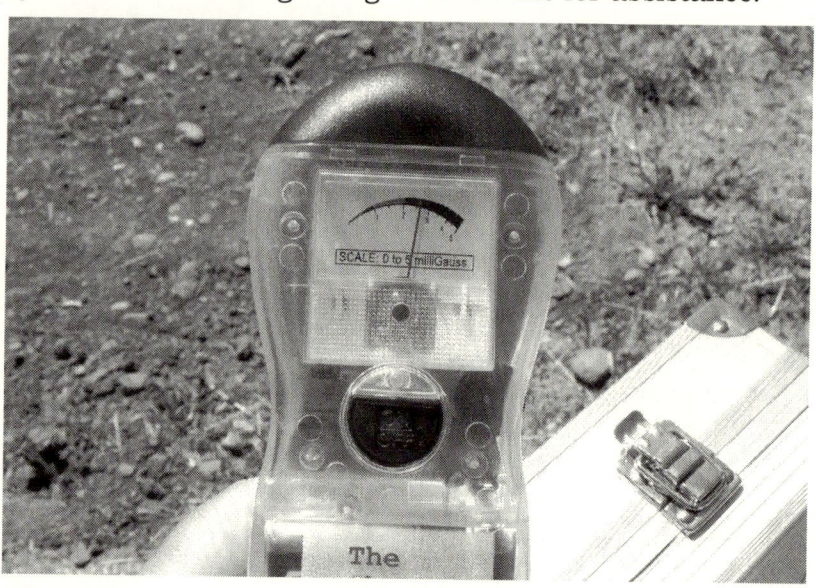

Soquel Cemetery, Soquel, CA

Months later my psychic friend, Tai Miller and I visited the Soquel Cemetery together. I brought them to the 18-year-old

Supernatural Santa Cruz - Second Edition
PART I: Haunted Sites

girl's gravesite, where I previously communicated with the young lady, and Tai confirmed that I helped her cross over into the light, where she is finally at peace.

Soquel Cemetery, Soquel, CA

Location: 550 Old San Jose Road, Soquel, CA 95073

Supernatural Santa Cruz - Second Edition
PART I: Haunted Sites

Supernatural Santa Cruz - Second Edition
PART I: Haunted Sites

CAPITOLA

The Capitola Village, CA. Photo by Sean Parola

The Rispin Mansion

Built in 1921, the Rispin Mansion was first owned by the wealthy Rispin Family, then became a Monastary and later a police dog training school. The mansion has been abandoned, dilapidated, and condemned since the 1970s. Its lack of upkeep seems to incubate more paranormal occurences from all its history. There are numerous spirits which haunt this eerie three-story building. Legend has it that anyone who lives there is cursed with losing all of their money.

The Rispin Mansion, Capitola, CA

The famous "Lady in Black," a Jesuit nun, makes her presence known more than any other ghost on the property.

Supernatural Santa Cruz - Second Edition
PART I: Haunted Sites

Several locals have experienced her paranormal antics, which include her full-body apparition appearing sporadically throughout the mansion. The nun has been observed standing in front of the top-story window looking down into the courtyard. She has also been witnessed reading a Bible in a rocking chair on the back porch. Some locals claim she has told vistors to, "Get out!"

The Rispin Mansion, Capitola, CA

Disembodied sounds of a dog barking and whining have been heard coming from the basement, also known as the dungeon. It is believed that this K-9 haunts the vincinty where he stayed when it was a police dog academy.

Supernatural Santa Cruz - Second Edition
PART I: Haunted Sites

Former entrance to the Rispin Mansion grounds, Capitola, CA

Back in the 1980s, after the house had been abandoned, a man fell through the floor boards three stories down to the basement. After crying for help for three days, he passed away from his injuries. Many have heard the spirit of a man cry out for help in the night. Other paranormal activity in the mansion includes hearing disembodied voices and screams, loud

Supernatural Santa Cruz - Second Edition
PART I: Haunted Sites

footsteps, windows and doors opening, as well as cold spots felt throughout this grandiose home. Some also attest to seeing the ghost of a man wearing glasses and holding a drink in front of the fireplace in the main room.

Additional Information:

- Some claim that a ghost greets you at the front door.

- It is alleged that murders occurred, along with satanic rituals, within this creepy dwelling.

- In October of 2012, my friends and I heard disembodied footsteps going down the cement pathway along the left side of the Mansion late in the night. We kept waiting to see who was walking toward us, but no one was there. The footsteps continued off and on for minutes, and sometimes it sounded like multiple footsteps.

- Using a Mel Meter device we picked up random spikes around the perimeter of the mansion.

Location: 2200 Warf Road, Capitola, CA 95010

www.rispinmansion.com

Supernatural Santa Cruz - Second Edition
PART I: Haunted Sites

The Shadowbrook

The Shadowbrook was once known as "The Haunted House" of Capitola before becoming a restaurant. The mansion was first built for Ernestine O. Fowler, a resident of San Francisco in the 1920s. It was used as his weekend getaway until 1940. The vacant quarters sat for five years before being bought, restored, and remolded into the Shadowbrook, which opened in 1947.

The Shadowbrook, Capitola, CA

While the haunted house was unoccupied, many neighbors alleged seeing strange things, along with having unusual and eerie experiences on the property. ". . . the presence of both a man and a woman have been seen," said Randall A. Reinstedt,

Supernatural Santa Cruz - Second Edition
PART I: Haunted Sites

California Ghost Notes. In recent years, apparitions and supernatural mists have been sighted in the enchanting restaurant after hours by former employees.

Objects are said to move on their own, such as doors and windows that shut regularly when the air is still. I spoke to an employee who said that he usually feels the presence of a male spirit while he's cleaning up at night on the bottom floor after closing for the night. The staff member alleged seeing napkins fly off the tables on their own occasionally. "I even saw it on the security camera one time," he stated.

The Shadowbrook, Capitola, CA

Supernatural Santa Cruz - Second Edition
PART I: Haunted Sites

The Shadowbrook, Capitola, CA

A bartender shared with me that a guest had an unexplainable encounter late one evening in 2011 when she was in the ladies room. The young woman entered the powder room, thinking she was alone, but while she was in the stall, the lights suddenly turned off and she heard footsteps walking toward her. As the unseen force reached the door of her stall, the woman then heard shuffling which abruptly stopped. She opened the stall to find no one there. The experience left her with a chill.

Supernatural Santa Cruz - Second Edition
PART I: Haunted Sites

One of the entities that has been sighted in the romantic and elegant establishment over the years just may be the friendly ghost of Fowler, who also haunts his old, charming estate.

The Shadowbrook, Capitola, CA

Location: 1750 Warf Road, Capitola, CA 95010

(831) 475-1511

www.shadowbrook-capitola.com

Supernatural Santa Cruz - Second Edition
PART I: Haunted Sites

The Capitola Theater

The late Capitola Theater, once an opera house, was built in 1948 and was recently demolished in 2009. Since the 1990s, there have been reports of supernatural occurrences throughout the building. The first report was from a construction worker who said that he heard a large crowd of people in the theater talking as if they were waiting for a show to start. As soon as he entered the room, the noise suddenly stopped and no one was there. Other workers have claimed to hear the same thing, but it only lasts for a few seconds, and then starts up again, reoccurring multiple times.

The previous owner, who passed away in 1997, was said to haunt the Capitola Theater. Her voice was heard throughout the building on several occasions. One time an employee was at the theater by herself when the phone rang. She heard a female voice yell from upstairs, "I'll get it!" When she went upstairs to investigate the voice she had heard, there was no one to be found. Although the theater no longer stands (a parking lot in its place) the ghosts are said to remain, still performing.

Location: Once stood at 120 Monterey Avenue, Capitola, CA 95010

Supernatural Santa Cruz - Second Edition
PART I: Haunted Sites

SANTA CRUZ

Harbor Beach, Santa Cruz, CA

Supernatural Santa Cruz - Second Edition
PART I: Haunted Sites

Coffeetopia

The coffee shop on Portola Drive in the El Rancho Shopping Center is believed to be inhabited by one or more spirits. I interviewed three employees who each claim to have had several unexplainable encounters within the building. Before the structure was converted into a coffee house in 1994, it was once used as a bank that was built in the 1970s. A large vault still remains in the shop and is used for seating. Johanna, a staff member, claimed that it scared her. "The first thing I do when I open up in the morning is turn the light on in the vault." I understood what she meant when I entered the room. The atmosphere felt a little heavy, especially in the entryway.

No one knows who truly haunts the building but some folks have theories. Within the last six months, the activity increased immensely after two customers named Steve and Nancy, who visited the shop daily, both passed away within a few months of each other. Steve was said to help set up in the mornings and pull out chairs. Amy, a staff member, said that since Steve's death chairs have been pulled out and moved on their own. Within the last few months she and Eli, another employee, have also witnessed "dishes flying off shelves" right before their very eyes. Recently, they heard the disembodied voice of former patron Nancy say, "Heelllooo."

Coffeetopia, Santa Cruz, CA

Supernatural Santa Cruz - Second Edition
PART I: Haunted Sites

Both Johanna and Amy have heard eerie sounds come from the attic and both agreed that one noise they both hear on occasion sounds like someone bouncing a ball on the floor.

They also feel as if they are being watched and followed around the shop on almost a daily basis. Johanna said that the radio has turned on all by itself and the volume is known to be turned up and down randomly.

Additional Information:
- Several years back, a former employee saw the ghost of an old woman in a Victorian dress inside Coffeetopia while unlocking the front doors one morning.

Location: 3701 Portola Drive, Santa Cruz, CA 95062

(831) 477-1940

www.coffeetopia.com

Supernatural Santa Cruz - Second Edition
PART I: Haunted Sites

Dominican Hospital

The 17-acre facility was opened in 1967 by the Adrian Dominican Sisters, assisting mass amounts of people every year, providing several different types of services. There have been thousands of deaths and births that have taken place at this hospital on the east side of Santa Cruz on Soquel Drive. The Intensive Care Unit (ICU) alone holds more than one thousand patients per year.

Not only is there residual energy that lingers from the births of babies, people passing, and even people who are in pain, there are ghosts who inhabit Dominican Hospital as well.

Over the years there have been stories of employees sighting ghosts of old nurses around the hospital.

Some employees talk about the mysterious "Phantom Baby cry" that's been allegedly heard by several Dominican engineers. Some claim to have heard the disembodied cries of a baby at random times around the hospital when there are no babies in the vicinity.

I spoke with an employee that I will call Jane. Jane has worked in the ICU for years and has seen and heard an abundance of spirits, mostly those who have just passed away in the prior Catholic Hospital.

"Within the first year of working in the ICU I began to have paranormal experiences. At first I didn't really accept or believe what was going on . . . until I had an experience of my own," Jane shared.

"A patient had died and it was one of the first deaths I witnessed at the hospital. I remember when he had just passed away, he was in the room to the left of me, and I was standing at the sink washing my hands. I thought to myself, 'Where is this person now?' Where is his spirit now?' And all of a sudden I felt something, like an energy just move through me. It walked through me from left to right . . . and it was him. It was one of the first forms of verification that I got," Jane stated.

"At the hospital I've seen shadows in the hallway and in the utility room, which was once used as a trauma room. For a long time, I couldn't be in there with the door closed because it was just really creepy, but after a while I started being more open to it.

"As far as full-body apparitions go at the hospital, I haven't seen any, but I have seen auras fade away to nothing from people who have just died, and I have felt some of them leave their body while I'm sitting next to them. I also receive images and messages in my head from former patients who recently passed," Jane explained.

Location: 1555 Soquel Drive, Santa Cruz, CA 95065
www.dominicanhospital.org

Supernatural Santa Cruz - Second Edition
PART I: Haunted Sites

Oakwood Cemetery

Founded in 1908, the Oakwood Cemetery, located in midtown Santa Cruz, definitely has a personality of its own. Located off the busy roads and freeway, the memorial park is surrounded by trees and an open field, occupied by critters and deer.

The Oakwood Cemetery, Santa Cruz, CA

Soon after I arrived at Oakwood Cemetery one night in 2011, I witnessed a pure black shadow person flying low to the ground from tree to tree for approximately three to four seconds. It appeared to be male, about six feet tall, and floated about four to six inches off the ground. I was able to see it clearly because of the back-lighting at the grounds keeper's home. Its features were so apparent, I could see its profile flying in front and behind the trees. This encounter gave me chills and made me experience extremely intense fear.

Oakwood Cemetery, Santa Cruz, CA

Upon recovering from this ordeal, I resumed setting up the equipment. Ten minutes later I saw another shadow person that looked a little bit different. The second dark apparition seemed to be touching the lawn when it traveled; I noticed the bounce in its walk. This entity also looked like a male and was in the same vicinty as the last, but was walking the opposite direction.

Supernatural Santa Cruz - Second Edition
PART I: Haunted Sites

It seemed to have shaggy hair that hung down low over its face; emanating a strong sense of sadness and despair.

Oakwood Cemetery, Santa Cruz CA

Additional Information:
- High EMF has been found around certain areas of the cemetery and EVPs have been captured.

Location: Paul Sweet Road, Santa Cruz, CA 95062

Supernatural Santa Cruz - Second Edition
PART I: Haunted Sites

Rossi's Body Shop And Towing Co.

Across the street from the old Holy Cross Cemetery, and in front of the additional graveyard, stands Rossi's Towing Company, originated in 1962. Over the years, employees have had unnerving and unexplainable paranormal experiences, and consider that the activity is due to the fact that the shop lies between two cemeteries.

Years ago, one employee heard what sounded like footsteps in the gravel past the door while he was working on a car late one night. Thinking it was an intruder, he got up suddenly but didn't see anyone. Another employee heard a disembodied voice coming from the side of the building one night and upon inspection didn't find anyone there. One tow truck driver claims that for years he has seen a dark shadow figure on the property periodically. Sometimes he'll see them walking through the yard, or standing near the front gate. Even with a bright porch light on, they'll allegedly show themselves on occasion. "Sometimes when I'm backing into the shop and I look into my rearview mirror, I'll see a shadow figure standing there near the gate."

Location: 203 Capitola Road Extension, Santa Cruz, CA 95062

Holy Cross Cemetery

The Holy Cross Cemetery was built in 1873 for the Roman Catholic community of Santa Cruz. Since the late 1800s, Holy Cross has been known to relocate remains. In 1885, six wagons carrying human remains were moved from Holy Cross Church on the Westside of Santa Cruz to the old Holy Cross Cemetery. The remains consisted of Ohlone Indians, Spanish soldiers, Yankee loggers and European immigrants. They were all buried together in one unmarked grave on the north side of the cemetery and still reside there today.

Holy Cross Cemetery, Santa Cruz, CA

Supernatural Santa Cruz - Second Edition
PART I: Haunted Sites

A few hundred yards away on 7th Avenue, sits the most recent addition to the cemetery, where the deceased have also been moved from one section to another. Some believe that the moving of remains can disturb the dead and lead to paranormal activity, such as hauntings.

The cemetery's most well-known phantom that passes through the old careworn grave yard, is the ghost of Jack Sloan (See Arana Gulch story). Since the 1950s, Sloan has been seen by multiple witnesses floating through the cemetery. Each year on the anniversary of his murder, Sloan's ghost is witnessed taking the same route through the neighborhood that he took over a century before.

Holy Cross Cemetery, Santa Cruz, CA

Supernatural Santa Cruz - Second Edition
PART I: Haunted Sites

On Halloween night 2010, I made a visit to the Holy Cross Cemetery. While I was walking around, I sensed something watching me from a gravestone nearby. I held up my camera and shot toward the direction I was sensing the spirit. Upon analyzing the dozens of photos I took, one really stood out. The aforementioned photo is shown below. There seems to be some kind of mystic fog or ectoplasm coming up from the grave.

Holy Cross Cemetery, Santa Cruz, CA
Note: The photo above has not been modified or edited.

In September of 2012, local psychic, Tai Miller and I visited the Holy Cross Cemetery together. Soon after we walked through the gates, Tai said she could "see" spirits sit up in their graves, look at us, and lie back down. This behavior continued as we walked through the cemetery past several sites.

Holy Cross Cemetery, Santa Cruz, CA

Location: Capitola Road Extension, Santa Cruz, CA 95062

Supernatural Santa Cruz - Second Edition
PART I: Haunted Sites

Arana Gulch

Nestled in the heart of Santa Cruz is the stunning Arana Gulch. It has been known to be haunted for decades by the Ghost of Jack Sloan (Andrew Jackson Sloan), who was shot and killed by Jose Rodriquez and Faustino Lorenzana on the evening of February 11, 1865 along the old Arana Bridge (located on Soquel Avenue, next to Jeffery's).

The north end of Arana Gulch, Santa Cruz, CA

According to local historian Phil Reader, the spirit of the 38-year-old has been seen on many occasions wearing a long, dark overcoat and a wide-brimmed hat, in or near the north end of the gulch. A member of the coroner's jury who investigated the

Supernatural Santa Cruz - Second Edition
PART I: Haunted Sites

killing said that this is what Sloan was wearing when he died. Sloan is known to appear on the anniversary of his death and has been reported by several eyewitnesses who spoke to S.C. Sentinel reporters regarding their encounters.

On July 25, 1895, 30 years after his death, a woman and her daughter were riding to town in their buggy when an apparition ran right out in front of them, and then vanished into thin air. Their description of the spirit and how it was dressed made the woman and her daughter believe that it was the ghost of Jack Sloan.

The second reported sighting was in 1913, by a large family who was living at the gulch at the time. The children came home to tell their mother about the new friend they had met in the gulch that day. They gave their Mother an exact description of Sloan. When he was 90 years old, one of these children verified the ghost story, also mentioning that his sister had seen Jack Sloan on several other occasions.

In 1932, the next sighting was reported. A family from out of town broke down on the side of the road when their car overheated. They claimed that a tall, thin stranger dressed in a dark overcoat came out from the bushes of the gulch and poured water in their radiator from the creek. To the driver's surprise, when he started cranking the automobile, he noticed that the stranger had faded back into the bushes.

Supernatural Santa Cruz - Second Edition
PART I: Haunted Sites

In 1953, a group of five boys also encountered the spirit late one night. The Boy Scouts observed the apparition "gliding as it merged with the woods."

The last Jack Sloan sighting was recently, when a couple that lives along the gulch came forward with their story. They said they often saw Sloan crossing their deck at night in front of their sliding glass door, generally accompanied with a low-lying fog.

Additional Information:
- Andrew Jackson Sloan is buried at Evergreen Cemetery, Santa Cruz, Calif.

Location: Agnes Street, Santa Cruz, CA 95062

Fuji Restaurant

During the turn of the century, the land where Fuji Restaurant now sits was once occupied by the Italian American Hotel. While it was used as an inn, legend has it that the mafia was known to hang out in the dwelling. Local historians also claim a murder took place on the property.

In the 1960s, Adolph's Restaurant was built in place of the hotel. This is when the ghost stories began to arise. There were reports of paranormal activity near the buffet, the kitchen and in the restrooms. Past employees alleged feeling and hearing the unnerving presence, as well as noticing objects move on their own, such as plates that were mysteriously being stacked in the kitchen, and some falling on the floor and breaking. Some individuals actually claimed to see the spirit and described him as a tall, dark male dressed in 40s attire with a long coat and hat.

I went to Adolph's in 1998 with a friend, without knowing any of its background or haunted past. As soon as we entered the building, I sensed it was occupied by a spirit. The air was oppressive, the atmosphere unearthly. My friend's mom happened to work there at the time, so I figured I should at least ask if anyone else felt an entity in the building.

"Is this place haunted?" I asked my friend.

"Yes! How did you know?" she asked.

"I can just tell," I said.

The unexplained activity went on and became more intense over time. It was then that the owners decided to get professional help to try and rid the place of the unsettling presence, so they contacted the Berkley Psychic Institute. It is not known if a psychic did indeed visit the restaurant, but the hauntings are claimed to continue to this day.

Adolph's closed a few years later, and the China 1 Buffet took over for a short period of time before being sold to the present owners who transformed the building into the Fuji Restaurant. Fuji staff claimed never to have spoken with former Adolph employees about the hauntings, but report seeing the same dark shadow man at times within the structure.

Supernatural Santa Cruz - Second Edition
PART I: Haunted Sites

Fuji Restaurant, Santa Cruz, CA

Location: 525 Water Street, Santa Cruz, CA 95060
(831) 427-0182

Callahan's Pub

Callahan's, the biker-friendly bar, opened its doors in the early 80s. The building, located on Water Street, was previously used as a bar and lounge called the Fireside Lounge. Over the years, the owner, employees, and guests have all experienced unexplainable phenomenon and believe with certainty that the pub is inhabited by spirits of old patrons and friends. Since memorials have been held in this establishment, it would make sense.

Callahan's Pub, Santa Cruz, CA

Strong spiritual forces and energy are felt throughout the pub. Ghosts have been sighted, and objects moved on their own. A coffee maker turned on after it was unquestionably turned off minutes prior.

Callahan's Pub, Santa Cruz, CA

I spoke with bartender Lete Goodwin who has been working at the bar since 2001. She and several others feel the energy of their past friends, customers, and acquaintances on a normal basis.

"This isn't a normal bar. This isn't a place where people just pop in; this becomes a second home for a lot of people. Some have infinite connections to this place, so when they do pass, the pub becomes an emotional tie for them. I have lost some good friends who would come here frequently, and I know they still do. I definitely feel taken care of at the end of the night," Lete stated.

One night when Lete went into the walk-in refrigerator, a customer saw the ghost of a man follow her in. As she came out and was closing the door, she said the customer told her to wait for the guy that was still inside.

"Honey, we're the only people here," Lete said to the patron.

At that moment, the customer realized that he had just seen a ghost.

"He got so freaked out, he just said, 'I got to go!' and took off," she exclaimed.

Additional Information:
- A former bartender has seen male spirits within Callahan's sitting at the bar and just standing around. And, on one particular occasion, she was followed half way home by one of them.

Location: 507 Water Street, Santa Cruz, CA 95060
(831) 427-3119

Santa Cruz Memorial

Malicious paranormal activity is believed to occur at night in the old, colossal Santa Cruz Memorial Cemetery. Built in 1862, this cemetery definitely holds the most history of any other cemetery in Santa Cruz County. Housing a mortuary and mausoleums with halls full of graves, it is said that some of the deceased roam the 25-acre property.

Santa Cruz Memorial, Santa Cruz, CA

The most common legends consist of seeing faces on tombstones, shadows stirring overhead, and hearing unearthly voices in the dark. Orbs can be seen by the naked eye, along with full body apparitions. Several ghosts that have been spotted tend to be wearing Victorian-style clothing or they look homeless. (There was a homeless camp next to the cemetery for years where many destitute people perished.) A ghost that has been seen most frequently is known to wear overalls and hold a shovel. Some locals believe he was once a groundskeeper for the cemetery.

Santa Cruz Memorial, Santa Cruz, CA

Some attest that spirits from the cemetery tag along and hitch rides with visitors back to their residences. Two locals claimed to have had the same experience several years ago. Ghosts followed them home from the cemetery and both of their houses were haunted for months afterward.

Supernatural Santa Cruz - Second Edition
PART I: Haunted Sites

Santa Cruz Memorial, Santa Cruz, CA

Location: 1927 Ocean Street Extension, Santa Cruz, CA 95060

Supernatural Santa Cruz - Second Edition
PART I: Haunted Sites

The Jury Room

The 1960s dive bar across the street from the court house on Ocean Street is said to be haunted by multiple spirits. I had honestly never heard anything about it being haunted, so I decided to find out for myself. I interviewed my friend, Brian Carey, who worked there for several years. During his shifts, he, as well as co-workers, managers, and past owners experienced unexplainable phenomenon and believed it was caused by the paranormal.

The Jury Room, Santa Cruz, CA

One of the ghosts who makes his presence known frequently is said to be the spirit of a former owner who occasionally still sits in the same place that he did while he was alive at the end of the bar. Brian and other employees have not only seen the foggy apparition from the corner of their eyes, but straight on as well.

Over the years, the atmosphere began to feel more eerie, and the hauntings increased, becoming more intense, especially after the early 1970s when the demented, local serial killer and necrophiliac, Edmund Kemper, visited the bar regularly. It is claimed Kemper would sometimes bring his deceased victims with him and keep them in the trunk of his car while he chatted with local police officers over beers. No one had any idea Kemper was capable of such ghastly behavior, putting behind them the fact that he murdered his grandparents when he was 15 years old. He secretly hoped that some of the officers he spoke with at the bar would figure him out, and when after his 10th nauseating murder they still hadn't, he turned himself in. His victims, the young, innocent female hitchhikers from around the county, are believed to haunt The Jury Room property. Sensations of sadness are felt at times, as well as the strong presence of one or more young female spirits.

The bar is also believed to be haunted by old patrons, whose ashes have been scattered on the roof of the Jury Room. Glasses are said to move on the bar, and doors open and slam close on their own, even when they are locked. Unexplainable drafts within the building cause objects to move on their own, too, such as an American flag, and dollar bills tacked to the ceiling.

Supernatural Santa Cruz - Second Edition
PART I: Haunted Sites

Individual voices and disembodied conversations have been heard, and unseen entities felt. Spirit orbs have also been sighted in the bar after hours by several former employees.

The Jury Room, Santa Cruz, CA

Location: 712 Ocean Street, Santa Cruz, CA 95062
(831) 426-7120

Supernatural Santa Cruz - Second Edition
PART I: Haunted Sites

Water Street Bridge

In May 1877, two men by the names of Francisco Arias and Jose Chamales were hung from the Water Street Bridge for being suspected of murder. It was known to be the last lynching of mixed heritage brought on by a mob of locals. Before these men took the leap to meet their maker, they were given a final shot of whiskey and said their last words.

Since the execution, people have claimed to see ghostly apparitions of the men near the bridge, sometimes hanging. Along with hearing footsteps, the bridge is known to cause eerie feelings of fear and dread.

Location: Water Street at River Street, Santa Cruz, CA 95062

Mission Santa Cruz

Mission Santa Cruz, 1791, Santa Cruz, CA. Public domain photo.

Built in 1791, The Santa Cruz Mission holds the legend of Father Quintana. The Father was known to beat and whip the Ohlone Indians while they were working at the mission, some as young as eight years of age. He was also said to sexually assault various women at the Mission. Quintana's cruelty got old fast. One dark, stormy night on October 12, 1812, Father Quintana was ambushed by the tribe. They could no longer bear his malicious acts. Some of the Ohlone tribe choked Father Quintana to death, while some crushed his testicles with rocks

Supernatural Santa Cruz - Second Edition
PART I: Haunted Sites

from the mission's foundation, and then they tucked Father Quintana was tucked neatly into bed.

Mission Santa Cruz, Santa Cruz, CA

Supernatural Santa Cruz - Second Edition
PART I: Haunted Sites

Mission Santa Cruz, Santa Cruz, CA

Supernatural Santa Cruz - Second Edition
PART I: Haunted Sites

Many believe Father Quintana's spirit still curses and roams the area, known as "Haunted Hill," trying to inflict pain and poverty on anyone he can. Witnesses claim his ghost has been seen dressed in a brown robe and sandals. Father Quintana is known to wander the historic landmark, stand at the altar inside the mission, and is even seen walking through the park across the street from the mission.

Santa Cruz Mission Park, Santa Cruz, CA

It is said that Father Quintana is buried underneath the Holy Cross Church located next to the Mission, although there is no grave marker.

Supernatural Santa Cruz - Second Edition
PART I: Haunted Sites

Holy Cross Church, Santa Cruz, CA

In 2011, I visited the Mission during the witching hour one night. I received responses on the Ghost Radar while using

Supernatural Santa Cruz - Second Edition
PART I: Haunted Sites

dowsing rods. I also recorded an EVP of some type of tribal drumming.

The second mission, adjacent to the original mission, built as a memorial of the first, Santa Cruz, CA

On the 200-year anniversary of Father Quintana's death, Sean Parola, Mat Weir, psychic Jena Reece, and I visited the haunted mission. Standing near the property, we believe to have spoken with both Indian spirits and with Quintana himself. Quintana's presence was strong; we sensed that he didn't want us there. When I asked if he'd like us to leave, the flashlight turned on. Not leaving quickly enough, an unseen force poked local psychic medium Jena Reece on her side, causing her much discomfort.

Supernatural Santa Cruz - Second Edition
PART I: Haunted Sites

While we were walking along the side of the Santa Cruz Mission, Jena saw the ghost of a middle-aged woman in a white gown walk across School Street and disappear before reaching the other side of the road.

Santa Cruz Mission, Santa Cruz, CA

Location: 144 School Street, Santa Cruz, CA 95060

Bocci's Cellar

The restaurant, bar, and bocci ball court was opened in 1925 by the Urbanis. The Italian immigrant family built the structure in 1885, and during their stay they lifted the house and built a large wine cellar. Bocci's Cellar's dining room and bar is located in this cellar, where astonishing paranormal activity is said to occur. Over the years, employees have seen ghosts, as well as witnessed objects moving on their own.

Bocci's Cellar, Santa Cruz, CA

One employee has seen the ghost of an old woman in the restaurant on more than one occasion, sitting in the back corner admiring a picture. The first time the staff member had this encounter, the ghost-woman's back was turned so he was unable to see who it was. It was after hours, so the employee figured it was a manager or one of the owners. The staff member approached the ghost and when he tried putting his hand on her shoulder, his hand went right through her body. It was at this moment that he realized this entity was no longer living. The mysterious, long gray-haired ghost, clothed in a Victorian dress, turned around and looked at him.

"She didn't have a face," he explained to me. The staff member saw her on a few other occasions always sitting in the same seat, admiring the Urbani Family photograph on the wall.

Bocci's Cellar, Santa Cruz, CA

Supernatural Santa Cruz - Second Edition
PART I: Haunted Sites

On a few occasions, the Urbani Family photograph was moved to another location in the cellar, and whenever it was, the activity would start up again. The phenomenon was obviously linked to this particular picture. When staff would put the aged photo back in its original spot, the ghostly activity would die down.

Photograph of the Urbanis at Bocci's Cellar, Santa Cruz, CA. Photo by Unknown. Courtesy of Bocci's Cellar, circa 1940s.

I was invited to investigate Bocci's Cellar after hours, so on October 13th, at 2:13 am, local psychic medium Jena Reece; Sean Parola, and I began our investigation. Within minutes there was paranormal activity. The Mel Meter, which measures EMF, began to spike randomly in the middle of the Bocci

Ballroom. We noticed the EMF increased as we walked toward the women's restroom. We stood in the middle of the restroom and asked the entity if they could please come closer to the device to make the numbers increase. Immediately, the meter started going up from 0.1 to 0.4 and then back down to 0.1 again.

Using the flashlight method with two mini Mag-lights, we were able to communicate with at least three different spirits. One was an old woman who was waiting for her loved ones to come home from the war, another was male, and the third was the little girl on roller skates in the old Urbani family photo. The spirits confirmed that the little girl still roller skates throughout the restaurant, and that some others are still playing bocci ball at the venue.

Location: 140 Encinal Street, Santa Cruz, CA 95060

(831) 427-1795

www.boccis.net

Evergreen Cemetery

Established in 1850, the Evergreen Cemetery is the oldest graveyard in Santa Cruz County. It is one of the very first pioneer cemeteries in California and is known to have paranormal phenomena at all hours of the night, and even in broad daylight. For decades, there have been claims of paranormal activity at Evergreen; apparitions and multi-colored orbs have been observed by visitors, high EMF (electro-magnetic fields) have been detected as well as rapid temperature fluctuations.

Evergreen Cemetery, Santa Cruz, CA

Evergreen Cemetery, Santa Cruz, CA

The ghost of an elderly woman has been observed in the Evergreen Cemetery on many occasions. Some allege to have observed her sweeping the top of the stairs in the back of the cemetery. One transient said that he saw her clear as day in front of an old shack on top of the stairs, yelling obscenities and telling him to leave. When the traveler went back years later, he didn't see the old lady or the rustic shack. Apparently, there never was such a shack, others told him later.

Evergreen Cemetery, Santa Cruz, CA

Additional Information:

- Years back, a woman claimed to have been grabbed by an unseen force through the bars of the crypt. She said the spirit would not let go. (Photo of crypt above.)

Supernatural Santa Cruz - Second Edition
PART I: Haunted Sites

Possible spirit apparition, Evergreen Cemetery, Santa Cruz, CA, 2012

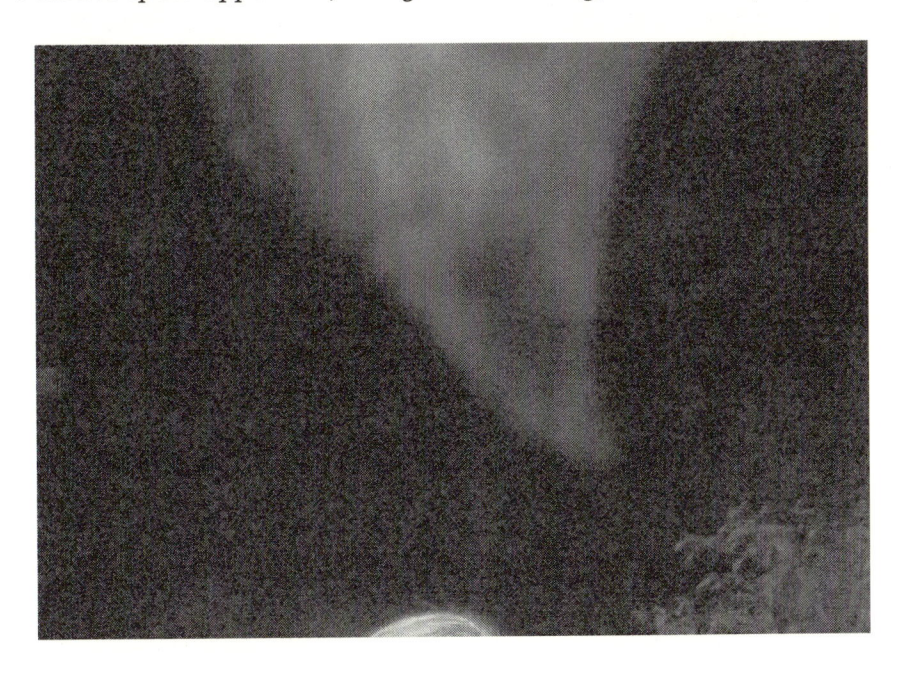

Supernatural Santa Cruz - Second Edition
PART I: Haunted Sites

Evergreen Cemetery, Santa Cruz, CA

Location: Evergreen Street, Santa Cruz, CA 95060

Supernatural Santa Cruz - Second Edition
PART I: Haunted Sites

Santa Cruz Main Post Office

This historical site was built in 1912. Over the years, the Santa Cruz Main Post Office has had additions, and was expanded in the 1930s and again in the 1960s. I interviewed a friend of mine, who I will call John; he worked for the post office for over 25 years. He said most of the paranormal activity that he and his co-workers experienced was in the most updated parts of the building.

"We never got a feeling of anger, or that something was trying to hurt us. It seemed more playful, like a 'Hello, I'm still here,' type of thing."

Supernatural Santa Cruz - Second Edition
PART I: Haunted Sites

"So, do you have an idea who haunts the post office? Do you know of any deaths that took place there?" I asked.

"There was a carrier that worked there for about 40 years who just loved working for the post office. About a month after his passing, the activity began, so we have always wondered if it was him," John replied.

John claimed that he and all of the other employees who worked graveyard shift started having unexplainable encounters in the parcel post area.

"You would get the feeling you were being watched. You turn to look and see something go by really fast out of the corner of your eye," he said.

On a nightly basis for several months, the graveyard crew saw bright white orbs of light, some as big as soccer balls, around the building.

"One of the guys was working alone in another area. We heard him yell and a garbage can fell over. So, we went over to see what was going on, and he said that he had seen one of those orbs. He caught it by surprise when he looked up and yelled, and the thing took off and knocked over a four foot garbage can before he watched the orb go straight through the wall."

Several employees also started having experiences in the eerie basement, so most of the staff didn't like to be down there alone. Cold spots were felt, as well as disembodied voices heard, such as a deep male voice saying, "Hellloooo."

"One morning I was putting my bike away, and I was the only one there at the time, when I felt someone tap me on the shoulder. I thought 'Who the hell is here?' So I turned around and no one was there," recounted John.

After months of experiencing paranormal activity in the post office, John claimed that the hauntings stopped abruptly.

Location: 850 Front Street, Santa Cruz, CA 95060

Supernatural Santa Cruz - Second Edition
PART I: Haunted Sites

The Vet's Hall

Veteran's Memorial (aka The Vet's Hall), Santa Cruz, CA

Built next to the main post office on Front Street stands the Veteran's Memorial Building, built in 1932. The historical landmark has always had an eerie feeling to it, especially in the basement.

In 2002, I went to a punk rock show down in the basement, and was one of the first to arrive. As I walked in, I noticed right away that the air felt heavy. While the first band set up their equipment, I felt lots of energy around the room, and wondered if it was haunted. Even after my encounter, I still wasn't sure what to believe. What gave me the incentive to even write this story is because last year I was told by an anonymous local that she also had unexplainable experiences in the basement. Hearing that someone else also had encounters in the same place, and at a different time confirmed my belief that the vicinity really is haunted.

"Back in the late 1960s my father would attend Fleet Reserve meetings there, and my mother belonged to a Women's Aux as well. While they were at meetings, my sister and I were sometimes left down in the basement alone. We went there once a month for years and years . . . I had some very weird things happen while we were down there."

It is not certain who haunts the Vet's Hall, but perhaps the building is haunted by some praiseworthy spirits with a strong sense of duty who served our country with honor.

Location: 846 Front Street, Santa Cruz, CA 95060
www.vetshall.org

The Red Room

The historic Victorian on Cedar Street was built in the late 1800s and was once used as a brothel, before being used as the Santa Cruz Hotel. Legend has it that a forlorn prostitute took her life by hanging herself in the building where the women's restroom is presently located in the restaurant. Her ghost, as well as others, are said to haunt the eatery and lounge.

Employees and guests have experienced very unusual encounters over the years, particularly when they are alone. Objects are said to move on their own, disembodied footsteps and voices have been heard, and apparitions have been seen.

"I heard footsteps as if someone had entered the bathroom. The footsteps got louder and it almost seemed as if someone was pacing back and forth in front of my stall. I looked under the door and realized there was no one else in the restroom other than myself." –Tina, Shadowlands.com

I spoke with a few employees who all believe the building is haunted and have each had an encounter.

"That's *so* weird," a waitress said to me when I asked about the haunting. "We were *just* talking about that."

The young employee had only been working at the restaurant for a little over a month but was well aware of its ghost stories.

A young bartender who I will call Marie, stated that she sees two spirits in her peripheral vision around the lounge area, usually around 4 am, when she's alone in the structure a few times a week.

Marie shared with me that a woman who looked to be in her late twenties wearing a long pale yellow Victorian dress has been sighted near both ends of the bar and in the kitchen.

"She's the one that appears the most . . . she's just kind of there observing everything," Marie said.

A young man in a brown three-piece suit and a top hat is the other spirit that's sighted most frequently, walking around the establishment and standing near the entrance of the lounge.

"I'm comfortable with them here. It's not negative; they're not being a menace, they're just here, like we're all existing together," Marie explained.

They do, on the other hand, like to get into a little bit of mischief at times.

"We'll get a lot of weird calls, especially right after I see the ghost with the three-piece suit. I answer and they'll hang up, or I'll answer and there's no one there at all; and that happens at least two to three times a week," concluded Marie.

The phantoms also like to move items, such as keys that have to constantly be replaced. "I'll hang up the keys, turn my back, look back, and they'll be gone," Marie declared with frustrated amusement.

Location: 200 Locust Street, Santa Cruz, CA 95060

(831) 425-1913

www.redsantacruz.com

The Del Mar Theater

Established in 1936, the old-fashioned, low-lit theatre, decorated with multi-colored lights and Victorian wooden carvings in the walls, takes you back to the 1930s. Over the years, there have been claims that the theater is haunted, and certain areas of the building feel as if a spirit inhabits the region. Former employees have heard unexplainable voices in the old dressing rooms, as well as seen dark shadow apparitions out of the corners of their eyes. The upper-level theater, where horror movies are usually played, also exudes abnormal energy at times. Two employees told me that that is where a lot of paranormal activity is said to occur.

The Del Mar Theater, Santa Cruz, CA

An old employee named Barney is said to haunt the Del Mar since his fatal heart attack while on the job in the projection room. Some staff members believe that the former projectionist causes all of the paranormal occurrences within the building. During the days of 35 mm film, the projectors at the theater were known to jam, the lights in the projection room would flicker, and seats in the auditorium are said to have flipped down by an unseen force.

"Now that the Del Mar switched to full digital projection, as of December 2011, the theater staff anxiously waits to see what

Barney will do now," said publicity manager Maurice Peel. - Quote from Santa Cruz Good Times, April, 2012.

The Del Mar Theater, Santa Cruz, CA

Location: 1124 Pacific Avenue, Santa Cruz, CA 95060

(831) 469-3220

www.thenick.com

The Asti

This aged, hip bar located on Pacific Avenue in downtown Santa Cruz was built around 1920. The structure was once used as a speakeasy called the Crossroads until 1937, when it became the Asti Café. It is believed that several uncanny events happened on the property before 1937, creating paranormal activity.

Employee Brian Carey, The Asti, Santa Cruz, CA

Over the years, employees have experienced the unexplained at the Asti Café, particularly in the basement where it once looked as if splatters of blood stained the walls. The basement was once connected to all of the underground tunnels of

Supernatural Santa Cruz - Second Edition
PART I: Haunted Sites

downtown Santa Cruz, where several homeless people, criminals, and bootleggers are said to have lived or passed through. Employee Brian Carey stated that the basement creeped him and other staff out so much, they literally just run in and out when they need to go down there. I spoke with a former employee who verified he would do it, too, and he's a big burly guy with tattoos.

"The ghost down there does not like me," the former employee stated.

The Pool Room, The Asti, Santa Cruz, CA

A former janitor claimed to have heard disembodied voices near the bar and pool room where a light hanging from the ceiling has been seen unexplainably swinging.

Supernatural Santa Cruz - Second Edition
PART I: Haunted Sites

Over the years owner Tara Gulielmo Muccilli had felt an unseen presence in the building, and never felt quite alone.

"I felt uncomfortable in the early mornings by myself," Tara explained. She said the feeling died down after the large windows were put in on the side of the building.

The Asti, Santa Cruz, CA

Location: 715 Pacific Avenue, Santa Cruz, CA 95060
(831) 423-7337

Supernatural Santa Cruz - Second Edition
PART I: Haunted Sites

Cliff Crest Bed and Breakfast

Nestled on Beach Hill, stands an historical Queen Anne Victorian once owned by the lieutenant governor of California. The quarters were built in 1887 for the governor William Jeter and his wife, Jennie. The Jeters both lived in the house until they passed away. Jennie outlived her husband by 29 years where she occupied a room now known as "Jennie's Room." This is the room in which she passed away.

Cliff Crest Bed and Breakfast Inn, Santa Cruz, CA

The ghost of Jennie Jeter has been experienced by many guests and employees for decades at the Cliff Crest Bed and Breakfast. Several witnesses have heard the sounds of footsteps, and of furniture being moved in her room, along with finding pillows that had been rearranged and put in disarray.

Jennie Jeter, early 1900s. Public domain photo.

Location: 407 Cliff Street, Santa Cruz, CA 95060

(831) 427-2609

www.cliffcrestinn.com

Supernatural Santa Cruz - Second Edition
PART I: Haunted Sites

The Santa Cruz Trestle

Built in the late 1800s, the Santa Cruz Trestle is believed by more than a few locals to be haunted by a number of spirits. Allegedly, over the years people have fallen or jumped off the bridge to their deaths. Several of them seem to stick around the vicinity. Some sensitives have felt the heavy residual energy at the bridge, left behind from lives being cut short too soon.

The Santa Cruz Trestle, Santa Cruz, CA

Two psychic friends of mine had uncanny experiences while walking the Santa Cruz Trestle at night.

"It's been a long time since I've been there. I felt a lot of uneasiness and like I was going to get pushed over. I felt very insecure. There's one energy that's the most prominent and there's this feeling like someone is playing a mean game, if that makes sense, like a bully. He has a dark, evil smirk, and is wearing a hat. He brings death, that's for sure. There's more than him; he's just the strongest and the loudest. The other spirits that are trapped there are afraid to come forward," my friend explained.

In 2012, I walked across the bridge with another psychic friend of mine. When we got to the middle of the trestle, he stood there in silence and looked a little uncomfortable.

"What's up?" I asked him.

"Someone is telling me to jump," my friend exclaimed.

Additional Information:
- The trestle is also known as "The Lost Boys' Trestle" after it was used in a scene in the film, *The Lost Boys*, 1987.

Location: Off Beach Street, Santa Cruz, CA 95062

Santa Cruz Beach Boardwalk

Photo by Debi Parola

The Santa Cruz Beach Boardwalk is known to be haunted by a 15-year-old boy named Walter Fernald Bryane. On September 21, 1924, Walter stood up at the end of the ride the Giant Dipper and fell head first onto the tracks. Attendants tried to stop the train, but Walter had already been crushed to death. He has been observed a number of times by employees and riders on and around the famous rollercoaster. He is usually witnessed at night after closing on the back of the train by ride operators while they're riding the giant dipper. Some employees claim to have seen Walter vanish into thin air toward the end of the ride. Tourists reported sitting next to a boy dressed in older clothing on the Dipper, and he vanishes sometime throughout the ride.

Along with sighting a full-body apparition throughout the years, ride operators have claimed to feel a tug on their sleeves when no one is in the area.

Santa Cruz Beach Boardwalk, Santa Cruz, CA. Photo by Debi Parola.

Supernatural Santa Cruz - Second Edition
PART I: Haunted Sites

Another haunted hot spot at the Santa Cruz Beach Boardwalk is the Cocoanut Grove. Most reports have been about poltergeist activity that goes on at the Grove after hours. Employees have claimed that chairs move around and get stacked on their own.

Cocoanut Grove, Santa Cruz Beach Boardwalk, Santa Cruz, CA

Supernatural Santa Cruz - Second Edition
PART I: Haunted Sites

Years ago, two staff members were scared out of their wits when they were closing up for the night. The employees were almost finished putting away the chairs when a mischievous spirit decided it wasn't closing time yet. As soon as they turned around, all the chairs were back in the seating areas and were stacked high and towering over them.

A friend of mine was a skeptic and never believed in ghosts until he became a security guard at the Boardwalk. Late one night, he and his co-worker heard a harmonica playing from inside the Cocoanut Grove. They knew the music couldn't have been made by anyone living because it had been closed for hours, locked up, and completely dark inside. As soon as they headed in, the harmonica playing stopped suddenly. Many employees and locals believe a ghost by the name of Woody haunts the Cocoanut Grove.

Location: 400 Beach Street, Santa Cruz, CA 95060
(831) 423-5590
www.beachboardwalk.com

Supernatural Santa Cruz - Second Edition
PART I: Haunted Sites

West Cliff Inn

The exquisite Italian Victorian overlooking the Boardwalk was built in 1877 by the Lynch Family. The home was known as the Lyncrest Manor during the Pioneer Era until the early 1920s, when it was used as a sanitarium run by a local woman by the name of Mary Jane Hanly. Miss Hanly had a reputation for having "mystical powers" and treated her patients using holistic remedies. She was said to have once revived a man after he had drowned in the ocean nearby. For years she was known as "The Mother of the Boardwalk" because of her love and compassion in helping others, as well as taking in people who were completely broke.

West Cliff Inn, Santa Cruz, CA

Supernatural Santa Cruz - Second Edition
PART I: Haunted Sites

In 1923, Mary Jane Hanly opened a hospital on the left side of the sanitarium, where surgical procedures were performed without any type of anesthetics or sedation. At times, murder victims were treated at the hospital, dying soon after being brought in.

In 1937, Miss Hanly became very ill and was bed ridden in the hospital where she died on August 31, 1937.

West Cliff Inn, Santa Cruz, CA

About a decade later the structure was transformed into a hotel and ghost stories began to arise. Local legends say a "lady in white" has been seen looking out the top window of the 3rd story. No one knows for certain whom the woman could be, but after investigating the West Cliff Inn, I believe it is the ghost of Mary Jane Hanly.

West Cliff Inn, Santa Cruz, CA

The first time I visited the hotel, the friendly manager, Matt Conceicao, happily showed me around the place and took me up to the room where the ghost has been sighted. As we began walking up the stairs, the energy began to intensify and the air got heavier with every step I took. When we reached the suite, which was once used as the attic, I felt immense pressure on my chest, and my palms began to sweat profusely. I quickly got out my K-2 Meter to find readings. Strangely, there was high EMF on top of the bed in the alleged haunted room. I moved the meter around to make sure it wasn't being affected by any type of electrical outlets or wiring (which it wasn't).

I spoke with a housekeeper who said that on one occasion, a couple was staying in a room below the attic and heard someone walking around above them throughout the night. The next morning, the guests told the staff members about their experience and were surprised to find out that the room had been vacant. No one had been staying in the suite during the disturbance, at least anyone among the living, anyway.

I returned a few days later to perform an investigation with Matt during the hours of darkness. During the investigation, we were unable to obtain any EVPs, but were very successful using the flashlight method. After speaking with the entity for almost an hour in the basement, and asking questions, such as who they were, when they died and how, we concluded that it was in fact Mary Jane Hanly who still haunts this land. When we asked her if she had magical powers, the light quickly turned on and shined brightly.

I tried convincing her to cross over, but she wouldn't.

Months later while walking past the inn with a few psychic friends of mine, they all immediately tuned into the residual energy left from the medical practices performed within the structure long ago. Both of them began talking to Mary Jane, trying to urge her to cross over, and to no avail.

Five months after that, I sensed her looking at the three of us as we were once again passing by, and both psychics said they saw her standing at the third story window of the West Cliff Inn waving at us.

Location: 174 West Cliff Drive, Santa Cruz, CA 95060

(800) 979-0910

www.westcliffinn.com

Yogi Temple

The mystical and outlandish "Court of Mysteries" made from brick and decorated with abalone and symbols, such as stars, was built by the eccentric Kenneth Kitchen in the 1930s. His brother Raymond also bought property down the road and began building his own bizarre quarters. It is said that each brother would only build at night by the light of the moon and a lantern.

In 1953, Kenneth Kitchen vanished and was never seen or heard from again. The property remained empty, unfinished and unkempt until it was bought by a pastor by the name of Father Karim in the 1960s, who converted it into St. Elias

Orthodox and Shrine. In the early 1990s it was left unattended and is still vacant to this day.

Yogi Temple, Santa Cruz, CA

Locals who live near the temple claim it is haunted, seeing strange, dark apparitions moving around the property at night. Others have heard unexplainable sounds while passing the numinous sanctuary.

The lot has been on the market for some time now, and a caretaker stays on the premises. I spoke with the care taker's brother who thought the place was "very creepy, especially at night."

Supernatural Santa Cruz - Second Edition
PART I: Haunted Sites

"So far I've only been here for about a week, and I'm almost convinced it's haunted."

The man claimed to see things move out of the corner of his eye, as well as sensing he was being watched. He has also heard eerie noises coming from inside the temple.

Inside the Yogi Temple, Santa Cruz, CA

Location: 519 Fair Street, Santa Cruz, CA 95060

- Note: The Yogi Temple is currently not open to the public.

Supernatural Santa Cruz - Second Edition
PART I: Haunted Sites

The Old Wrigley's Building

The famous Wrigley's chewing gum factory was established in 1892. Their former location on Mission Street is the largest building in Santa Cruz County, and was built in 1955, and used until 1997. While the factory was still in commission, workers wondered if the building was haunted after countless unexplained experiences.

One employee claimed to have seen the ghost of a man inside the main warehouse. It was early one morning and he believed to be the only person there until he saw a figure out of the corner of his eye walk past him. He thought it was just his co-worker until he heard a door that was locked open, and he watched as the ghost walked through the door. It wasn't until that very moment that this local decided Wrigley's really is haunted.

Location: University Business Park, 2801 Mission Street, Santa Cruz, CA 95060

Wilder Ranch

Before this historic ranch was used as a dairy farm, the land was known as Rancho Arroyo del Matadero, and later on named Rancho del Refugio. The property was occupied and used by Ohlone Indians as slaughtering grounds for cattle until 1854, when a man by the name of Moses Meder bought the land and created a dairy farm.

In 1871, The Wilder family took over the ranch and created a new and updated creamery. For almost a century, the Wilder Family resided on the land and maintained the business until 1969. In 1974, it was taken over by the California State Parks.

Several of the aged houses and ranch-style buildings from the mid to late 1800s still stand on the property today, keeping the old-time spirit alive. I spoke to a docent at the ranch and asked if she had ever heard of any ghost stories or sightings that had taken place there.

"We do have a resident, but he's only seen on certain days," the elderly woman, dressed in Victorian attire, replied. She also senses energies around the ranch, particularly inside the Wilder's former house. I agreed that I had felt an abundance of energy in this old dwelling as well, especially in one of the small bedrooms on the bottom floor; it was almost overwhelming to stand in the room for those couple of minutes while we were given a tour.

Wilder's Victorian House, Wilder Ranch, Santa Cruz, CA

Supernatural Santa Cruz - Second Edition
PART I: Haunted Sites

The historic Cow Barn, Wilder Ranch, Santa Cruz, CA

Built in 1850 by previous rancher Moses Meder, The Cow Barn is one of the oldest structures on the property. In 2012, a family had a paranormal encounter while approaching the old barn. The children ran ahead of their parents into the barn but quickly dashed out screaming, claiming that they had just seen a ghost. In disbelief, the children's father, Bill, walked into the barn. He saw a shadow figure standing against on of the walls.

"That's what the kids must have been freaking out about. I went closer to check it out. The shadow moved toward me and that's when I realized this was something supernatural. I took a step back and the shadow moved to the back and disappeared right through the wall," Bill, Ghosts of America.

Supernatural Santa Cruz - Second Edition
PART I: Haunted Sites

The historic Cow Barn, Wilder Ranch, Santa Cruz, CA

Location: 1401 Old Coast Road, Santa Cruz, CA 95060

(831) 423-9703

www.parks.ca.gov

Red, White and Blue Beach

Red, White and Blue Beach, Santa Cruz, CA

Red, White and Blue Beach is known for its ghostly goings. It is documented that when the beach was open to the public, dozens of campers, locals, and tourists had unexplainable encounters there and nearby. One of the oldest legends that has been told by locals for generations is about "the window that doesn't exist." While walking the beach late at night, many guests say they have seen a window lit up on the hill overlooking the water. Witnesses have described the window as cathedral-like. Some claim to have even seen movement and full body apparitions pacing in front of the ghostly window. As the sun rises, there is no house to be seen – just an empty hill.

The ghost of a Sea Captain is witnessed by dozens of people every year at Red, White and Blue Beach. He is seen standing on the hills overlooking the water, walking along the shore, or hanging around The Edward House, which is also known to be haunted by his spirit. (See The Edward House story.) He's recognized by his old black rain slicker, cap, and boots, along with his solid, vintage-looking appearance. Many have reported observing the Sea Captain strolling around the camp grounds as if he were flesh and blood, and then suddenly disappears.

Additional Information:
- A woman was murdered on the beach by her boyfriend. It is said that her ghost haunts the vicinity as well.

Location: 5021 Coast Road, Santa Cruz, CA 95060
www.redwhiteandbluebeach.com

- Note: Red, White and Blue Beach is currently not open to the public.

University of California, Santa Cruz

The Henry Cowell Ranch, now located on the UCSC campus, was owned by the Cowell Family back in 1850. The family lived in this historic home, called the "Cowell House," from 1865 to 1897. In 1897, the family moved up to San Francisco, where Henry Cowell died six years later. Only six months after Henry's death, Henry and Alice Cowell's second to youngest child of five, died tragically on the ranch while visiting her Mother. The woman's spirit is said to have haunted the town for over a century.

On May 14, 1903, 40-year-old Sarah Agnes Cowell took a trip down to the old Cowell Ranch, where she liked to pick wildflowers. Sarah and the housekeeper were riding a high-spirited horse and buggy across the fields together one day when disaster struck. One of the wheels from the buggy hit a rock, scaring the horse, making it bolt. Tragically, Sarah Agnes flew from the buggy and broke her neck, killing her instantly.

Sarah's spirit still haunts the Ranch and has been witnessed on many occasions in 'The Haunted Meadow,' also located on the UCSC campus. The first detailed sighting of Sarah's spirit was reported to the Sentinel in 1975. One night in 1971, a group of students were wandering the meadow, when her ghost frightened one of them beyond belief. The student ran back down the trail and met up with the group alleging to have heard distinct footsteps behind him when there was no one in sight.

The remains (two wheels) of Sarah Cowell's buggy, Santa Cruz, CA

In 1973, Sarah was spotted in the upper quarry on the UCSC Campus. A student claimed to see her transparent, cloaked spirit casting an eerie shadow beneath the quarry. The local legend of Sarah Cowell's spirit has been told from generation to generation, likely keeping her spirit alive.

MISS COWELL MEETS DEATH IN RUNAWAY

Daughter of Millionaire Accidentally Killed Near Santa Cruz.

Mrs. Frank George, Her Companion, Receives Severe Injuries.

Horse Becomes Frightened and Dashing Along Rough Road Throws Occupants of a Cart Out on Pile of Rocks.

Special Dispatch to The Call.

SANTA CRUZ, May 14.—Miss Sarah Cowell of San Francisco, a daughter of Henry Cowell, the millionaire lime and cement dealer, was killed this morning by being thrown from a cart on top of a pile of stones. Her friend, Mrs. Frank George, was badly injured and is in a critical condition. Miss Cowell had been visiting Mrs. George, whose husband is superintendent of the Henry Cowell Lime and Cement Company. The George family resides in the old Cowell home, where the millionaire's daughter was born.

Mrs. George and Miss Cowell left in a cart for an outing this morning, and were above the upper kilns, which are about six miles from this city, when the accident happened. The road at that point is very steep, rough and rocky. Just how

San Francisco Call article, 1903

Another ghost by the name of Lily appears in 'The Haunted Meadow.' Legend has it that the beautiful young transient woman lived in the field in the 70s and died there. Lily's apparition has been seen a countless number of times walking around the vicinity in either rags, or completely naked.

The Haunted Meadow, UCSC Campus, Santa Cruz, CA

On the third floor of Building B at Porter College, occupants have complained over the years of suddenly awakening in the night, feeling as if someone was strangling them. The bottom floor of Building B has been condemned because of reoccurring paranormal incidents. There have been several reports made of objects flying across rooms, random noises, such as voices heard incessantly, along with malicious feelings and energies. The ground floor is known as "The Bermuda Triangle."

The last notorious haunting on the University's Campus also took place in Porter College, but in Building A. Years ago, a student hung himself on the fifth floor. It is alleged that he has been occasionally seen walking down the halls of the building. Multiple eye witnesses claim to have seen him in dark pants and a white shirt.

Porter College, Building A, UCSC Campus, Santa Cruz, CA

Supernatural Santa Cruz - Second Edition
PART I: Haunted Sites

The Cowell Carriage House, UCSC, Santa Cruz, CA

"The road up to the University past the entrance is haunted by the ghost of some type of old timer. He looks like a working man from I'd say about a hundred or so years ago, way before they built the campus. I have seen him and so have others I've spoken to. He appears briefly at the side of the road at random times it seems."

-B Slug, Ghosts of America

Additional Information:
- Sarah Agnes Cowell has been seen in the shadows of the trees, mostly in the afternoon or before twilight. She is known to be wearing a long, pale yellow dress and a bonnet.

Supernatural Santa Cruz - Second Edition
PART I: Haunted Sites

- Henry Cowell owned a limestone and cement company on the property, which could have amplified the residual hauntings that took place. Paranormal researchers believe that limestone retains history. It is believed that ghosts are attracted to the energy in these sedimentary rocks, and tend to reside in these types of dwellings.

Remnants of the historic Henry Cowell Lime Kilns, UCSC, Santa Cruz, CA

Location: 1156 High Street, Santa Cruz, CA 95060
(831) 459-4003
www.ucsc.edu

Pogonip

According to local lore, "The Ghost of Pogonip" has been haunting the Pogonip vicinity ever since this Indian man was sentenced to death by his tribe for standing up to his elders. With his dying breath, he cursed the tribe and swore to haunt them for eternity. Many believe his curse on the tribe and on the area is the cause of strange deaths and peculiar events in and around Pogonip.

Pogonip Park, Santa Cruz, CA

It is known that there are sacred Indian burial grounds covering the area, many claiming that bones and skulls litter

Supernatural Santa Cruz - Second Edition
PART I: Haunted Sites

the vicinity underneath the soil. Several locals and visitors said that they saw spirits throughout Pogonip, along with hearing footsteps and chanting.

Additional Information:
- The Pogonip Clubhouse was used as "Grandpa's house" in the motion picture *The Lost Boys*, (1987). The house still stands today and is known by numerous locals as "The Lost Boys House."

"The Lost Boys House," (Pogonip Clubhouse), Pogonip, Santa Cruz, CA

Location: 333 Golf Club Drive, Santa Cruz, CA 95060

Supernatural Santa Cruz - Second Edition
PART I: Haunted Sites

DAVENPORT

Saint Vincent De Paul Catholic Church

Saint Vincent De Paul Catholic Church, Davenport, CA

This allegedly haunted Catholic Church was built in 1915. For generations, many locals have witnessed apparitions coming and going from the church. Some have observed anywhere from one to dozens of ghosts leaving the building at a time. Some locals who have seen this activity believe that the devoted religious spirits left some kind of imprints on the church. Sometimes they are seen in broad daylight, looking as if they are departing from a funeral or Sunday Worship. It is said that the ghosts are most often witnessed on dark, overcast mornings.

Saint Vincent De Paul Catholic Church, Davenport, CA

Location: 123 Marine View Avenue, Davenport, CA 95017

Waddell Creek

In 1875, a man by the name of William Waddell was walking through the forest on his land with his hunting dog when they got too close to a mama bear and her cub. The bear attacked Waddell and mangled his arm so severely that it had to be amputated. The arm was buried in the north coast meadow. Shortly after Waddell's passing, the mourners set off to unbury his limb for the funeral, but the arm had disappeared.

Waddell Creek, Davenport, CA. Public domain photo by unknown.

Ever since the arm's disappearance, people passing through Waddell Creek will mysteriously lose their belongings. Random items tend to go missing in the area, and Waddell's arm is always to blame. Stagecoach drivers would warn their passengers, while passing through the vicinity, to keep their possessions close and to watch out for "the sticky fingers of William Waddell's arm," according to a Metro Santa Cruz article in 1999.

Gravesite of William Waddell, Santa Cruz Memorial, Santa Cruz, CA

Location: Off Highway 1, Davenport, CA 95017

Supernatural Santa Cruz - Second Edition
PART I: Haunted Sites

Supernatural Santa Cruz - Second Edition
PART I: Haunted Sites

SANTA CRUZ MOUNTAINS

Mystery Spot

The Mystery Spot was discovered in 1939, and was opened to the public in 1940 for touring. This particular location is definitely bizarre. It is known as a gravitational anomaly, where the law of physics does not apply. Some think it's all an optical illusion. Others consider there is a vortex at the Mystery Spot creating the abnormal surroundings and generating a supernatural portal to another dimension. Many employees, locals, and researchers believe that long ago an alien spacecraft crashed into the mountains in the vicinity of the Mystery Spot, causing all of the weird anomalies at the park.

"Most of us here believe there's a large alien spaceship underground and the motor is still going in circles, and that causes the large gravitational pull that makes us lean." This is quoted from a Mystery Theater film, investigating the Mystery Spot on Dailymotion.com. It is said that the ghosts of the aliens who died in the crash haunt the vicinity of the Mystery Spot.

Many of the Eucalyptus trees located around the attraction are twisted into corkscrew shapes. Normally Eucalyptus trees grow straight with small bends here and there. A theory that some scientists have is that the trees are trying to counteract the pull of the Mystery Spot.

Mystery Spot, Santa Cruz, CA

As well as other phenomena, the majority of cameras have a hard time focusing in the cabin to take pictures and to record videos. Camera's batteries are known to drain quickly when inside the slanted house, too.

A Mystery Spot staff member stated that there was an elderly man who used to come to the attraction once or twice a week because it made him feel younger. The visitor claimed that he would take in the energy waves that are created by the Mystery Spot, and that this energy gave him "oomph." Several others notice that their migraines go away when they reach the cabin.

Over the years, people have claimed that the attraction is haunted, and that ghosts are drawn to the gravitational pull. Some have claimed to see bright, colorful, glowing orbs around the Mystery Spot at night.

Location: 465 Mystery Spot Road, Santa Cruz, CA 95065

(831) 423-8897

www.mysteryspot.com

Supernatural Santa Cruz - Second Edition
PART I: Haunted Sites

Highway 17

Highway 17 is known to be one of the most dangerous roads in California. The twenty-six-mile, winding route makes its way through the mountains from Scotts Valley to Los Gatos, California. For generations, many drivers and passengers have reported seeing apparitions walking and/or standing along the highway, and some have even seen them sitting in the back seats of cars. Others have alleged seeing white vaporous clouds floating over the lanes. Some have claimed to see the ghost of a 17-or 18-year-old girl walking along the road at twilight. Along with seeing spirits wandering the area, visitors driving through sharp turns have heard sounds of collisions and tires screeching to a halt, and upon inspection, and no reckless drivers at the scene.

Additional Information:
- The apparition of an Ohlone Indian man has been seen for centuries walking on the side of the highway. Legend has it he causes all the accidents on Highway 17.

Location: The main highway that connects Santa Cruz to San Jose, CA

Supernatural Santa Cruz - Second Edition
PART I: Haunted Sites

Pine Knoll Pet Cemetery

The Pine Knoll Pet Cemetery is tucked away in the hills next to Highway 17, nestled in between residences on Sims Road. The animal burial grounds are claimed to be haunted by beloved pets, which many have buried here since the 1940s.

Pine Knoll Pet Cemetery, Santa Cruz, CA

Numerous visitors claim to have had paranormal experiences in the graveyard. The deceased pets are known to roam the cemetery at night, barking, howling, meowing and crying, and have been distinguished as dark, shadow-like apparitions.

Supernatural Santa Cruz - Second Edition
PART I: Haunted Sites

Pine Knoll Pet Cemetery, Santa Cruz, CA

Location: Sims Road, Santa Cruz, CA 95060

Supernatural Santa Cruz - Second Edition
PART I: Haunted Sites

Graham Hill Road

The long, windy road that runs parallel to Highway 17 that leads you up to the Santa Cruz Mountains and the San Lorenzo Valley has a rich history. Over the years, many people have died in horrific car accidents on Graham Hill Road, usually due to drinking and driving or speeding. Some of the events have made such a mark in our dimension that residual energy lingers on the narrow two-lane road.

For decades, people have claimed to witness the ghost of a young woman walking down the road at night near the south end, usually walking north. Many speculate that she either died on the road, or that she is walking from Santa Cruz Memorial from up the road. Some confuse this woman with the notorious "White Lady" of Santa Cruz. (For White Lady's story see Private Residences).

Sensitives can feel the residual energy that lingers up the road, particularly when they are passing the south end of Henry Cowell State Park. Some have had the sense of panic and fear. Psychics have envisioned the horrific accidents that have occurred for years. Driving north, you may notice all of the memorials on the right side of the road.

While residing on Graham Hill Road, an old psychic friend was visiting one morning when she saw the apparition of a teenage boy standing in my bedroom looking at us. She said that he was tall and thin, dressed in 80s attire.

"He was wearing a yellow hoodless sweatshirt, jeans and white tennis shoes. I'm pretty sure he died in a car accident in the 80s on Graham Hill Road," the psychic shared.

"Does he want something from me?" I asked.

"No, I don't think so," she went on. "I think he just comes and visits you sometimes."

While driving down the street using the Ghost Radar application on my phone, I have picked up dozens of words and responses. Graham Hill seems to have the most paranormal activity than any other road in the County, I've noticed.

It has picked up words such as, Help, Ghost, Stop, Road, Drive, Car, Transportation, and names such as, Edward, Ben, Ann, and Dan.

Location: Graham Hill Road, Santa Cruz/Felton, CA

Supernatural Santa Cruz - Second Edition
PART I: Haunted Sites

The San Lorenzo River

According to legend, the town's first Caucasian visitor was a shipwrecked sailor who wasn't accepted by the Indians. The tribe saw him as an intruder and sentenced the sailor to death. One of the tribe members warned the sailor of his tribe's intentions, and when his clan found out, they condemned him to death as well. With the Indian traitor's last breath, he vowed to haunt his people forever. The "Spirit of the San Lorenzo River" is said to have terrorized the Indian tribe until he divested them all of their happiness and content lives.

The San Lorenzo River, Santa Cruz County, CA

Supernatural Santa Cruz - Second Edition
PART I: Haunted Sites

Additional Information:

- This ghost story was first recorded in print 120 years ago in the Santa Cruz Sentinel.

- Indian burial grounds cover the area and old human remains are still found to this day.

The San Lorenzo River, Santa Cruz County, CA

Location: Off Highway 9, Santa Cruz to Boulder Creek, CA

Santa Cruz Mountain Tunnels

The tunnels in the Santa Cruz mountains are known hot spots for ghost hunters. Two tragic incidents occurred in the tunnels under Highway 17, killing 32 workers. The first horrific event took place in 1879 at the Laurel and Wright tunnels. There were two gas explosions that blew some of the miners to bits making it impossible to recover the remains of each victim. Many of the workers' remains are still there today, more than 100 years later, now buried beneath the soil. The other disastrous incident occurred only a year later in May of 1880. A train travelling at high speed flew off the tracks, and more than half of the 125 passengers were thrown from the railroad, killing 15 and severely injuring 50.

Supernatural Santa Cruz - Second Edition
PART I: Haunted Sites

A drawing of the 1880 train wreck, public domain photo

It is believed that these two catastrophic occurrences are what caused paranormal activity to transpire. Legend has it that the ghost workers have been haunting the tunnels since soon after their horrifying deaths. The first documented report was in 1890 and printed in the local newspaper, where a Santa Cruz resident spoke of seeing 30 ghosts walking out of the Wright Tunnel.

Many ghost hunters have observed orbs, light anomalies, apparitions, and EVPs from the tunnel's entrances. Sounds of screaming, crying, and moaning have been recorded by various ghost seekers. Other paranormal enthusiasts have captured amazing EVPs of what sounds like the "ghost train" near the Laurel Bridge, where no active trains currently travel.

The Laurel Tunnel, Santa Cruz, CA

Location: Laurel Road at Schulties Road, Santa Cruz Mountains, CA

Supernatural Santa Cruz - Second Edition
PART I: Haunted Sites

FELTON

Roaring Camp Railroads

Nestled in the redwoods, Roaring Camp Railroads has a long history. Before Spanish explorers came to the vicinity in the 1700s, where Roaring Camp now stands on Bear Mountain, it was once inhabited by the Zayante Tribe. In the 1830s, a lodger named Isaac Graham settled in the area, which was later named Roaring Camp. Isaac also constructed Graham Hill Road for his lodging company so that he could easily commute to Santa Cruz and back.

In 1875, the city began giving rides to passengers on the steam engines from the mountains to the beach. The pleasant Roaring Camp Railroads is now a preserved piece of history from the 1880s. The park has an old western appearance, making visitors feel as if they have gone back in time when the trains first began to run.

Roaring Camp's Jane Doe, a 125-year-old, headless female skeleton was found on Bear Mountain located in Roaring Camp off of Graham Hill Road in 1996. Some workers were clearing the brush and saw their dog playing with a human bone, which led them to the corpse that still had remnants of clothing and items from the early 1870s. The skeleton was found wearing a leather vest, a loaded .32 pistol revolver, a knife, gold coins, a gold watch, glasses, and a bottle of liquor. Her death looked as if it had been caused by a .44 bullet shattering the lower-left portion of her rib cage. The bullet was lying underneath the skeleton when it was found. Her hands and feet were missing, along with her head, all believed to have been taken by animals. Could this courageous woman's spirit still be occupying the woods of Felton?

Her remains were buried at Evergreen Cemetery in Santa Cruz, CA, with a headstone that reads:

Gone to the Golden Hills
The Unknown Clamper

Died Circa 1890
Buried with Honors, 1998

In recent years, hikers found human remains near the tracks at this historical landmark. The corpse was never identified and specialists couldn't predict whether it was a man or a woman because the pelvic region was missing. There have been no leads on how this person was killed.

Whoever it was, though, is definitely trying to reach out and make their presence known. Ever since the body was found, trains keep stalling on their own during all hours of the night right where the corpse was found. Conductors claim to have repeatedly observed a woman crossing the tracks. As soon as they make the train come to a screeching halt, there is no one in sight. In 2009, a conductor claimed to see strange lights and shadows.

Supernatural Santa Cruz - Second Edition
PART I: Haunted Sites

Roaring Camp Railroads, Felton, CA

Location: 5535 Graham Hill Road, Felton, CA 95018

(831) 335-4484

www.roaringcamp.com

Felton Covered Bridge

Built in 1892, the Felton covered bridge is said to be the tallest bridge in the United States. The 180-foot-long bridge was used as the main entrance into Felton from Santa Cruz until 1937. In 1957, it was registered as an historical landmark, and still stands within the Covered Bridge Park located on Graham Hill Road.

Felton Covered Bridge, Felton, CA

Ghost are known to be attracted to conduits, such as bridges, tunnels, railroad tracks, rivers, streams, and creeks because of the energy they create. Ley lines are said to have haunted hot spots as well, and certain kinds of minerals such as limestone and crystals are known to magnetize spirits.

Supernatural Santa Cruz - Second Edition
PART I: Haunted Sites

Limestone is known to be scattered around Santa Cruz, particularly in the mountains. Located over a river, this bridge has its share of paranormal activity, so I felt that it would be a place for us to investigate.

Felton Covered Bridge, Felton, CA

After investigating the bridge on two separate occasions, I concluded that it is haunted by at least one spirit, a woman who claims to have been murdered on the bridge long ago for being a witch. I was able to communicate with her using the flashlight method, as well as with a pendulum and the Ghost Radar.

Location: Covered Bridge Park, Graham Hill Road at Mount Hermon Road, Felton, CA 95018

Monty's Log Cabin

Every time I've gone past Monty's Cabin in the last decade, I've always had a sense it was haunted. I had never visited the bar before, until the night of December 3, 2011. As my friend Jane and I walked into the country-style tavern (decorated with deer heads) I immediately noticed the paranormal energy in the cabin. After looking around, appreciating its cool mountain-man décor, Jane sat down at the bar next to an elderly gentleman who seemed a bit tipsy. I once again felt something, almost as if it were right behind me.

I turned to Jane and said, "This place is totally haunted, dude."

She smiled.

Before she could respond, the man sitting next to us overheard me and said, "I've never seen you two here before."

"Yeah, this is my first time, and Jane's third time," I said.

"So you've never been here, you just walked in and you claim it's haunted?" he inquired.

"Yes!" I said with confidence.

"And you never heard of it being haunted?" he asked.

"No, I just know it, dude," I said.

The man immediately leaned over the counter and shouted across the bar to the owner, "Hey, Monty, is this place haunted?"

"Yeah, it is!" said Monty. "George is still here!"

Supernatural Santa Cruz - Second Edition
PART I: Haunted Sites

The man at the bar looked back at me in drunken amazement.

"Wow, you were right!" he exclaimed.

Monty's Log Cabin, Felton, CA

Monty walked over to us and explained who George was, filling us in on all of the activity they have encountered. He said George's spirit is still very active, and that he and all staff members make a point to acknowledge George's existence.

George was the bar's previous owner from the 1970s to the early 1990s. Known for his great sense of humor, he died a little before his time due to Multiple Sclerosis in the early 1990s. Ever since, George's presence has been felt within the bar.

Supernatural Santa Cruz - Second Edition
PART I: Haunted Sites

Doors are said to open and close on their own, along with lights turning on and off on their own.

A bartender said that she had actually yelled at George a week ago after he kept turning off the lights. She had to turn them back on multiple times throughout the evening, and the only explanation was that George was up to his old tricks again.

The owner explained how he and a couple of customers witnessed a cup of beer fly off the counter when there was no one near it. This was unusual behavior because George's spirit is said to be very pleasant. Monty believes that George did it because he didn't like the woman whose drink it was.

Monty's Log Cabin, Felton, CA

Every night before closing up the bar, a staff member sets out three chairs in front of the front door for their visiting ghosts

Supernatural Santa Cruz - Second Edition
PART I: Haunted Sites

George, his sister Rose, and a past staff member named Pat. One night a staff member forgot to leave the chairs out. That night the bar was broken into.

I went to the car and grabbed the K-2 Meter. Soon after I turned the EMF detector on, it started to spike. While sitting at the bar, the lights rose and stayed on for a matter of seconds before suddenly stopping. I got up and walked around to see what could be setting it off. The juke box seemed to give off a little EMF along with the neon signs in the windows, but the meter wasn't spiking nearly as high as it did minutes after I had first turned it on. We left the device on during our visit and noticed huge spikes here and there. None of the spikes seemed consistent. What made our mouths drop was when a song came on and I jokingly started to dance and sing; it seemed as though George started to join in using the K-2 Meter. The lights on the EMF detector were lighting up, increasing and decreasing to the beat of the song. It went on like this for almost two minutes. It looked very much like an Audio Spectrum Analyzer on a stereo.

"Wow, he's having fun," said Jane.

We were both amazed and baffled. We had never seen anything like it before. I very much regret not bringing my video camera into the bar. We could feel his energy becoming very strong, almost as if he were standing at the bar with us, rocking out to the music.

Being there that night just felt right, which was rather odd since I very rarely go to bars. Later, I realized why the name

Supernatural Santa Cruz - Second Edition
PART I: Haunted Sites

George kept popping into my head a couple of weeks earlier. I thought of the name so much while Jane and I were investigating the Boulder Creek Cemetery, I said aloud to Jane, "I keep thinking the name *George*." Either George was trying to make contact with me or I picked up on the fact that we were going to visit him. Either way, it happened.

Location: 5575 Highway 9, Felton, CA 95018
(831) 335-9969

Felton Cemetery

The aged cemetery originated in the 1870s, and many of the graves are from that era. For the most part, the graveyard gives off a very welcoming and calm vibration, almost like being at Grandma's house. Though, there is one area, on the right side of the cemetery, where the energy is a little unsettling. High EMF has been found around the area, and possible spirit orbs have been caught on camera during the hours of darkness.

Felton Cemetery, Felton, CA

Some of the spirits who dwell in the vicinity are open to communication. Disembodied footsteps have been heard, and cold spots felt. Some people have even claimed to have been touched by unseen forces.

Possible spirit orbs in Felton Cemetery, Felton, CA

One night, while Jane, Sean, and I were investigating the cemetery, I asked the spirits if they could finish the last two knocks from the tune *Shave and a Haircut*. I knocked on the gazebo, waiting to hear the "two bits." Immediately, two uncanny knocks were heard.

While using the flashlight method to communicate with the spirits, one of them claimed to be an old soldier from World War II, and he seemed to be manipulating the light, possibly using Morse code.

Supernatural Santa Cruz - Second Edition
PART I: Haunted Sites

"Are you using Morse code?" I asked.

The light stopped blinking and shined brightly.

In late 2012, we returned to the cemetery with a local psychic. During our visit, she saw the full-body apparition of a sailor dressed in a blue uniform standing just to the right of us several yards away. He stood there staring at us before vanishing. We approached the area where he had been, and sure enough, we found a grave marker for a young sailor.

Location: Love Street off Felton Empire Road, Felton, CA 95018

Fall Creek

Nestled deep in the mountains of Fall Creek, covered in ivy and moss, stands the I.X.L. Lime Company ruins, originated in the mid 1870s. Henry Cowell bought the company in 1900, and it was used until 1919. The intense heat of the kilns at 1,700 degrees Fahrenheit, and the sounds of the loud blasts upset locals who lived in the area; it was common for workers to hear people yelling and cursing at them for making their habitat so uncomfortable.

Lime kiln ruins, Fall Creek, Felton, CA

My friend Morgan and I spoke with a spirit using the flashlight method at the ruins one afternoon in May of 2012.

Supernatural Santa Cruz - Second Edition
PART I: Haunted Sites

The spirit claimed to be a young, white male who died on the land, and told us that he would like to reunite with his family. Morgan began to experience unexplainable feelings of sadness. "When you first started calling on them, it felt like people were all around us," he announced.

Lime Kiln Ruins, Fall Creek, Felton, CA

Shortly after visiting Fall Creek, I looked into its history and found that a 33-year-old Italian man by the name of Grossi Gotardo died there after a fatal accident in 1891. Gotardo and James Kirby, another worker, were crushed by rocks, severely injuring Kirby and killing Gotardo. Gotardo's skull was crushed as the ledge gave out. He left behind his wife and three children

Supernatural Santa Cruz – Second Edition
PART I: Haunted Sites

in Italy. With this information, I can't help but wonder if Morgan and I spoke with Gotardo, their histories being so similar.

Walking along a trail near the kilns, Morgan pointed out a certain area to me that is believed to have a portal or vortex to another dimension. It was once marked by bent trees, creating an arch over the entrance. He wouldn't go near the area, though. After he had walked through one similar in a different location months prior, it just didn't feel right.

In 2009, a psychic had a supernatural experience near the kilns as well.

"All of a sudden I saw it.... About fifty feet in front of us, I saw a large orb of energy – about five feet in diameter. It appeared as a distortion in the atmosphere like a ripple or like what happens when you view an object through a water bubble."

-Charles Peden, Psychic, Medium
Quote from www.charlespeden.wordpress.com

Location: Off of Felton Empire Road, Felton, CA 95018
(831) 335-4598
www.santacruzstateparks.org

Supernatural Santa Cruz - Second Edition
PART I: Haunted Sites

BEN LOMOND

Supernatural Santa Cruz - Second Edition
PART I: Haunted Sites

Highlands Park

The twenty-six-acre park along the San Lorenzo River in Ben Lomond, California, was named by the property's original owners, Lord and Lady Anderson, who resided on the land in the early 1900s. Lord Anderson named his property "The Highlands" in honor of his rich Scottish Heritage, and sold the land soon after his wife died.

In the late 1930s, the Nasser family bought the land and built the house that still stands today, surrounded by Highlands Park. The Nasser family was known to throw parties as they loved to entertain guests in their old home.

Highlands House, Highlands Park, Ben Lomond, CA

Supernatural Santa Cruz - Second Edition
PART I: Haunted Sites

In 1977, the county opened a recreational area, naming it Highlands Park, in memory of Lord and Lady Anderson.

Just walking around the property, some sensitives can feel the strong residual energy that lingers. It is said that ghosts haunt the old, well-kept 1930s house and its surroundings. Doors in the kitchen are said to unexplainably swing open by an unseen force, as if someone is walking in and out of the room.

"Pretty harmless, but entertaining nonetheless." –Highland Joe, Ghosts of America website.

In October 2012, my friends and I were headed down to the river behind the property and stopped to use the public restroom in front of the house. When psychic Tai Miller , walked out of the bathroom, she saw the ghost of a woman in a dress standing on the balcony of the Highlands house. The woman looked at us for a moment until she saw that she was noticed, and then went back into the house. Tai sensed that the woman had once owned the house.

"She's not interested in communicating," Tai said.

Location: 8500 Highway 9, Ben Lomond, CA 95006

Love Creek

A little past midnight on January 4, 1982, tragedy struck in The Ben Lomond Mountains. A massive landslide that was estimated to be 500 yards wide and 700 yards long crashed down on dozens of homes overlooking Love Creek. A witness recalled seeing "the trees snap like toothpicks" along with others who saw homes filled with mud, and cars completely buried with mud and trees, falling into the creek below.

Love Creek, Ben Lomond, CA

The horrific mudslide ended up killing ten people. Some were never found. Valley Churches United Missions established an agency in honor of the tragedy. They have lists of the missing

Supernatural Santa Cruz - Second Edition
PART I: Haunted Sites

people who were never located. Along with their names, phone numbers are attached from loved ones trying to find their long-lost family members and friends.

Locals and neighbors allege seeing the apparitions that didn't make it that tragic night wandering the area of Love Creek. Some believe the spirits are trying to uncover their lost bodies.

Love Creek, Ben Lomond, CA

Supernatural Santa Cruz - Second Edition
PART I: Haunted Sites

Love Creek, Ben Lomond, CA

Location: Love Creek Road, Ben Lomond, CA 95006

Supernatural Santa Cruz - Second Edition
PART I: Haunted Sites

BROOKDALE

Supernatural Santa Cruz - Second Edition
PART I: Haunted Sites

The Brookdale Lodge

The Brookdale Lodge, AKA Brookdale Inn and Spa, Brookdale, CA

Supernatural Santa Cruz - Second Edition
PART I: Haunted Sites

Located in the deep, dark Santa Cruz Mountains stands the famous Brookdale Lodge, built in 1903. It is said to be one of the most haunted locations in California. The recently renamed Brookdale Inn and Spa, is claimed by psychics and locals to be inhabited by 49 spirits, who decided to never check out. It is also believed that there are portals and vortexes around the lodge, allowing spirits to come and go as they please.

During the 1940s and 1950s, the Lodge was home to many local gangsters. Legend has it that they would bury bodies underneath the floors, leading to livid ghosts with bad intentions creating havoc around the hotel.

The Brookdale Lodge, Brookdale, CA

The Brookdale Lodge's first owner, Judge James Harvey Logan, is believed to haunt the vicinity. Psychics, including

Sylvia Browne, claim to have made contact with him. After communicating with Logan, he allegedly slimed Browne with ectoplasm.

Judge James Harvey Logan, circa 1900. Public domain photo.

Legend has it, around 1912 Logan lost his young niece, Sarah, while she was playing on the property one day. It is said that Sarah slipped and fell to her death in the creek located on the property.

Little "Sarah Logan" has been seen more than any other spirit in the lodge. Over the years, there have been countless sightings of her ghost, witnessed by visitors and employees alike. She is known to be seen in a blue and white Victorian-style Sunday dress near the fireplace in the lobby, running around the fireside room, playing in the brook, or throughout the halls and on the balconies of the Brook Room. Some claim to have approached Sarah, speaking to her as she cried for her mother. When the eye witnesses look away, Sarah vanishes.

Another ghost who has been seen by many is speculated by psychics to be Sarah Logan's mother, or her nanny, Maria, who is believed to be looking for Sarah. This spirit is mostly seen in the Brook Room as well. The smell of Gardenias often permeates the room at night, although there are no Gardenias throughout the haunted lodge. Several people who experienced the paranormal phenomenon assume that the smell is from her.

The Brook Room is identified to have the most paranormal experiences throughout the hotel. Many have claimed to hear glasses, plates and silverware clinking, along with footsteps, voices and even conversations from dozens of ghostly diners. Some have even caught ghosts on film. Recently, a couple ran out of The Brookdale Lodge when they reviewed their digital images and saw a ghost in the background. It has been reported that fully-charged cell phones and cameras go dead quickly, likely from ghosts drawing the energy from any source they can.

The Brook Room, Brookdale Lodge, Brookdale, CA

The Mermaid Room is another hot spot in the lodge. Some have stated that they witnessed the ghost of a man standing at the bar having a drink long after closing. Visitors and employees have experienced hearing whispers, voices, clinking glasses, and soft music when the Mermaid Room was completely empty. The jukebox is known to turn off and on, and glasses and chairs move on their own. One never feels completely alone in this room.

The Mermaid Room, Brookdale Lodge, Brookdale, CA

The Pool Room is believed to be haunted by the thirteen-year-old girl who allegedly drowned in 1972, forcing the pool's closure. The long, browned-haired girl has been seen on occasion floating face down in the water or standing around in the Mermaid Room. Guests have complained about feeling cold spots randomly, in accompany with getting touched by unseen forces. Some claim to have encountered hearing the teen speak quietly, and have seen splashing in the pool when it was vacant.

The Kitchen is said to have constant phenomenon, from pots and pans swinging and banging around to shadow-like figures that fly about. An article from the Santa Cruz Sentinel dated January 9, 2008, states that a Chef claimed to have seen a heavy cooking pot full of water do a full rotation on one of the burners. He said that the doors to the kitchen also swing open and closed, as if someone has been walking through them.

In the bar, there is usually some story going around about the most recent haunting. Bartenders at the Lodge are aware that they don't just clean up for the living. They clean up after the dead as well, when glasses and bottles fly and slide off shelves.

Additional Information:
- Room 13 was changed to room 12 A, because of complaints that it was haunted.

- Employees and locals believe that the hauntings have increased tremendously since the Lodge recently changed owners.

- The Lodge has been visited by many famous people such as, President Herbert Hoover, Mae West, James Dean, Marilyn Monroe, Shirley Temple, and Tyrone Power.

Supernatural Santa Cruz - Second Edition
PART I: Haunted Sites

The Log Cabin Room, Brookdale Lodge, Brookdale, CA

Additional Information:

- Room 13 was changed to room 12 A, because of complaints that it was haunted.
- Employees and locals believe that the hauntings have increased tremendously since the Lodge recently changed owners.

- The Lodge has been visited by many famous people such as, President Herbert Hoover, Mae West, James Dean, Marilyn Monroe, Shirley Temple, and Tyrone Power.

Supernatural Santa Cruz - Second Edition
PART I: Haunted Sites

Location: 11570 Hwy 9, Brookdale, CA 95007

(831) 338-1300

www.brookdaleinnandspa.com

Supernatural Santa Cruz - Second Edition
PART I: Haunted Sites

BOULDER CREEK

A vintage postcard of downtown Boulder Creek, CA. Public Domain Photo by Unknown.

Boulder Creek Cemetery

Only one hundred sixty nine graves are accounted for within the Boulder Creek, I.O.O.F. Cemetery. At least four of the headstones are made of wood, and three of them are illegible. Several of the gravesites have cracked or missing tombstones, which isn't surprising since the cemetery is said to date back as early as 1862.

Boulder Creek Cemetery, Boulder Creek, CA

The Boulder Creek Cemetery has had its share of paranormal activity. Dark shadow people have been seen meandering late at night in the eerie cemetery on occasion, and rapid and drastic temperature fluctuations have been noticed.

Supernatural Santa Cruz - Second Edition
PART I: Haunted Sites

I investigated the cemetery in 2011 and received amazing results and believe to have made contact with a child named Constance.

Boulder Creek Cemetery, Boulder Creek, CA

The ghost of a woman in a yellow jumpsuit has been witnessed sitting on a bench across the street from the cemetery by visitors, neighbors, and children from the nearby schoolyard. Students have pointed out the woman to teachers who were unable to see her.

Location: Harman Street, Boulder Creek, CA 95006

Supernatural Santa Cruz - Second Edition
PART I: Haunted Sites

The Late White Cockade

Deep in the woods of Boulder Creek sat the White Cockade Scottish Pub. Built in 1930, the pub was known to be haunted by its first owner Barbara Stanford. This haunted pub was so eerie that some customers were known to come once and never go back again. The latest owner claimed that one customer actually screamed in fright and ran out of the building after experiencing paranormal activity within the walls of the old hostelry. Many witnesses have said they saw Barbara's pale ghost in and around the pub when it was in operation.

The White Cockade, Boulder Creek, CA

Supernatural Santa Cruz - Second Edition
PART I: Haunted Sites

In 2006, after her uncanny supernatural experience, Nancy Palajac was convinced that Barbara's spirit was trying to communicate. Nancy found the garland she had recently mounted on the floor with the tacks neatly stacked on a chair. Psychics say she's harmless and protective of the place, though she was known to be quiet the prankster. When there was an annoying customer at the pub, sometimes their bar stool would suddenly slip out from under them.

Additional Information:
- Some say the Pub was being shared by ghosts. Another spirit that some believe resided there was a logger named Ben, who died in the 1980s.

- Lights and stove burners were known to turn off and on by themselves.

- Footsteps were heard in unoccupied rooms followed by Barbara Stanford's apparition.

Location: 18025 Highway 9, Boulder Creek, CA 95006

- Note: The White Cockade was closed down in 2010

```
Supernatural Santa Cruz - Second Edition
    PART II: Confidential Locations
```

Supernatural Santa Cruz - Second Edition
PART II: Confidential Locations

PART II:

Confidential Locations

```
Supernatural Santa Cruz - Second Edition
   PART II: Confidential Locations
```

Supernatural Santa Cruz - Second Edition
PART II: Confidential Locations

PRIVATE RESIDENCES

The Sunshine Villa, Santa Cruz, CA

Supernatural Santa Cruz - Second Edition
PART II: Confidential Locations

White Lady's

The White Lady's house, 1959, courtesy of the Graham Hill Water Treatment Plant, Santa Cruz, CA

The Legend of the "White Lady" of Santa Cruz has been told for more than a century, and her ghost has been seen by an abundance of eye witnesses. Recently demolished, the empty lot where the White Lady's cottage once stood is known to have countless numbers of paranormal occurrences. The White Lady is also notorious for haunting the surrounding areas, such as down Ocean Street Extension, and on occasion she has been observed at the Santa Cruz Memorial Cemetery at the end of the road.

Supernatural Santa Cruz - Second Edition
PART II: Confidential Locations

According to legend, it all started back in 1870 when a German fellow sent away for a mail-order bride from Massachusetts. Shortly after his young, beautiful bride arrived, they got married and settled down in the stone cottage, now known as "White Lady's." Legend has it that the "old lush" got drunk nightly and forced his bride to wear her wedding dress, and then he would beat her ruthlessly. When the bride decided to leave her husband, he found out about her plan and made sure she didn't follow through with it. He beat her to death, decapitated her, left her body in the house, and set their home ablaze. Despite the legend, the first reported fire of the stone cottage was in 1970. "White Lady's" burned to the ground leaving it roofless, only the four, thick, stone exterior walls left standing.

Soon after the bride's disappearance, "hordes of people," as stated in a Santa Cruz Sentinel article, began reporting seeing a glowing ghost wearing a wedding gown floating around the area. She was also seen looking out the top window of the abandoned house before the fire. In the 1970s, White Lady's became a huge drinking and make-out spot for teenagers. Various locals claim to have seen The White Lady in her blood-soaked wedding dress with her head tucked underneath her arm.

"Her gown is bloody and her hair is wool-looking, and she has been heard mumbling, 'Get out of here before I kill you.' My father told me the story as a young boy and I of course did not believe it, until I saw her myself." –J. Crowder, Strange USA

White Lady's house, 1999, Santa Cruz CA

The author at White Lady's, Santa Cruz CA, 1999

Supernatural Santa Cruz - Second Edition
PART II: Confidential Locations

One dark night in April 2011, I went by the deserted lot to take photos. I was standing in the middle of the road on Ocean Street Extension facing the property. It was so dark I couldn't even see my hand in front of my face. It was dead silent except for the crickets that seemed to chirp in sequence. All of a sudden, the temperature dropped and I could hear footsteps walking toward me on the gravel. The footsteps sounded as if they were only a foot or so away when they stopped. I spun around and took off running to the car.

I returned to the vicinity near White Lady's months later with my friend Mel and our friend, Sara. When we first arrived, we sat in the car and Mel read aloud the legend of the White Lady from my first book, *Supernatural Santa Cruz,* to get into the mood and to let Sara in on the story behind it.

We began asking if anyone was there that would like to speak with us. Mel and I both felt a strong female presence come toward us. We sat the flashlight down and within a minute or so it turned on and off by itself. We asked the White Lady to turn it off for us and she did each time we asked.

I misplaced my recorder, but after finding it, we noticed that the Ghost Radar picked up the word "Record," and the flashlight had turned on at the same time.

The following are some questions we asked using the flashlight when the White Lady's answers were *Yes.*
Mel: Were you murdered?

Supernatural Santa Cruz - Second Edition
PART II: Confidential Locations

Mel: Did your husband murder you? If your husband murdered you, can you turn the light on?

Just to verify, Mel repeated the question.

Mel: Is that a yes? If your husband murdered you, can you turn the light on really bright?

The light got brighter a moment later.

Mel: If your husband used to beat you, can you turn the light on?

Mel started to feel a cold spot near her.

Sara: Maybe you need a new flashlight. Maybe something is wrong with this flashlight.

Mel and I laughed.

Me: All right. We have a skeptic here. Can you please turn on the light and make it flash on and off for us?

It did as I asked.

Mel: Can you do that again for us, please?

It flickered once again.

Mel: Did you die in your wedding dress?

Mel: Can you turn the light on really bright if your husband killed you in your wedding dress?

The light got extremely bright and wouldn't turn off. (She was having way too much fun making the light flicker.)

Mel: Did your husband beat you to death?

Right then the Ghost Radar picked up the word, "Entirely," and the flashlight came on immediately afterward.

We heard noises around us in the woods and asked the White Lady to verify that it was just animals. The light came on.

Mel: Have you been here a long time?

Me: Are you stuck here?

Me: Are you stuck on this property?

While filming Mel, I saw an orb float by her that was very similar in size and direction as the orb I caught on film at the Brookdale Lodge.

Me: Do you want us to help you? Do you need help?

The Ghost Radar picked up the word, "Writing."

Mel: Did you used to be a writer?

Me: Maybe she's referring to the story I wrote in my book about her.

The flashlight turned on, literally, a second later.

Me: Are you happy I wrote about it, making you famous?

The light came on bright for three seconds and then turned off.

Me: Have people seen your spirit here?

Mel got out her pendulum and started using it to contact the ghost. You can use one to communicate with spirits by letting them move the weight and swing it horizontally or vertically.

"Does your name start with the letter *B*?" Mel asked.

The pendulum started swaying vertically for, "No."

"Does your name start with the letter *C*?"

It then started swaying horizontally for, "Yes."

Supernatural Santa Cruz - Second Edition
PART II: Confidential Locations

Just then a car drove by, their stereo blasting Nekromantix, a Psychobilly band Mel and I both love. As I enthusiastically pointed it out, the spirit tugged on the pendulum while Mel was holding it. It can actually be seen on the video footage. I captured it being pulled down by an unseen force and then springing back up.

"Wow!" Mel exclaimed. "She just tugged on my pendulum!"

"Do you not like that music?" I asked. "Can you turn the flashlight on if you didn't like that music?"

The flashlight quickly turned on.

"We like it. Sorry."

"So, your name begins with the letter *C*?" Mel asked.

The pendulum started swaying horizontally once again.

"Can you turn on the flashlight if your name starts with a *C*?" I asked.

The flashlight turned on immediately.

It was getting late and soon it would be time to go.

"Would you like us to come visit you again sometime?" I asked.

The flashlight turned on and shined very brightly for about six seconds and then slowly turned off.

Before we left, I took pictures of the front of the property. The first photo I took appeared to have a few anomalies in it, while the photos I took only seconds later were covered in colorful orbs. I had never seen such an amazing orb photo. (See photo below and photos on the next two pages.)

Supernatural Santa Cruz - Second Edition
PART II: Confidential Locations

The first photo I took at White Lady's, when asking the spirit to show herself. You will notice hardly any strange anomalies in the photo.

Immediately afterward, I took a second and then a third photo, both capturing a bunch of possible spirit orbs.

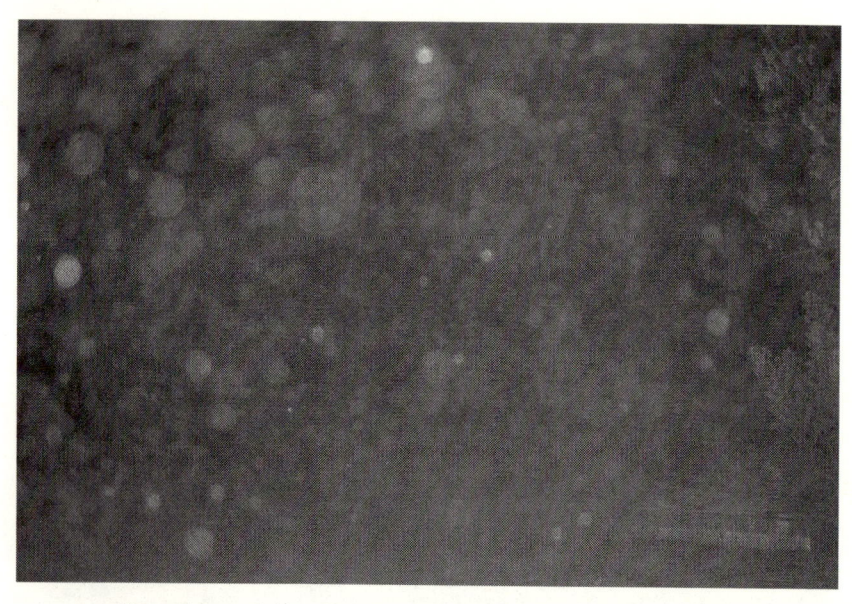

Supernatural Santa Cruz - Second Edition
PART II: Confidential Locations

Possible spirit orbs, White Lady's, Santa Cruz, CA

Mel sent the orb photo above to two psychics. Neither psychic lives in town, and neither knew our story, or the

Supernatural Santa Cruz - Second Edition
PART II: Confidential Locations

possible dark history involved. One of them is a photo psychic, which means that he can see events and get impressions and/or feelings just by looking at a photo. When he first looked at the photo, he said that it was one of the most legitimate spirit orb photos he has ever seen. He truly believes the orbs were made by a ghost. The psychic also said that he could see a woman standing in the photo wearing a dress with flowers in her hair. When the other psychic reviewed the photo, she saw a woman with flowers in her hair wearing a dress as well. She picked up that a woman was killed there by her husband, either by getting hanged or getting her throat slit. She wasn't positive on how the White Lady was murdered, but she said it had something to do with her throat. This psychic believes the marriage was arranged and felt sadness while gazing at the photo.

Location: Ocean Street Extension, off Quail Crossing, Santa Cruz, CA 95060

The Golden Gate Villa

The Golden Gate Villa was built in 1891 by Major Frank McLaughlin. It is recognized that the home was also assembled on sacred Indian burial grounds. McLaughlin married a woman with a three-year-old daughter named Agnes, and soon after he married her Mother, he adopted Agnes as his own. As time went on, Agnes grew into a beautiful young lady, who was known to rarely date. After a while, rumors spread through the town that Frank and Agnes were having a romantic relationship.

The Golden Gate Villa, Santa Cruz, CA

Supernatural Santa Cruz - Second Edition
PART II: Confidential Locations

Major Frank McLaughlin, circa 1900. Public domain photo.

Agnes McLaughlin (center with guitar), circa 1900s, courtesy of the Golden Gate Villa

On the second anniversary of Agnes's mother's death, McLaughlin had a horrific arrangement that he regretted soon afterward. On November 16, 1907, at the ripe age of 34, Agnes came home one day and loosened her corsets to lie down in bed. Major Frank McLaughlin (57 at the time) entered her room, and without any hesitation, shot Agnes in the temple with a .44 caliber handgun. McLaughlin then took a fatal dose of cyanide, taking his own life along with his adopted daughter's. It is claimed that the Major's motive was clearly because of his guilty passion for Agnes. It is confirmed that in McLaughlin's last letter he wrote, "I love her so, and so I take her with me."

Supernatural Santa Cruz - Second Edition
PART II: Confidential Locations

The Golden Gate Villa, Santa Cruz, CA

After Agnes's death, a large, jeweled, stained-glass window was made in her honor. A few strands of Agnes' hair were also placed in the glass. Legend has it that Agnes still haunts the old Victorian quarters. The present owner stated that "Agnes's ghost still wanders the house," and a former owner feels like she's being watched, especially while she's cleaning the home, according to a Metro Santa Cruz article on October 29, 2003. The Villa's owner believes that McLaughlin never had eyes for Agnes, loving her only like a daughter. Sometimes if you're lucky you'll catch a glimpse of Agnes's spirit standing around or drifting throughout the mansion.

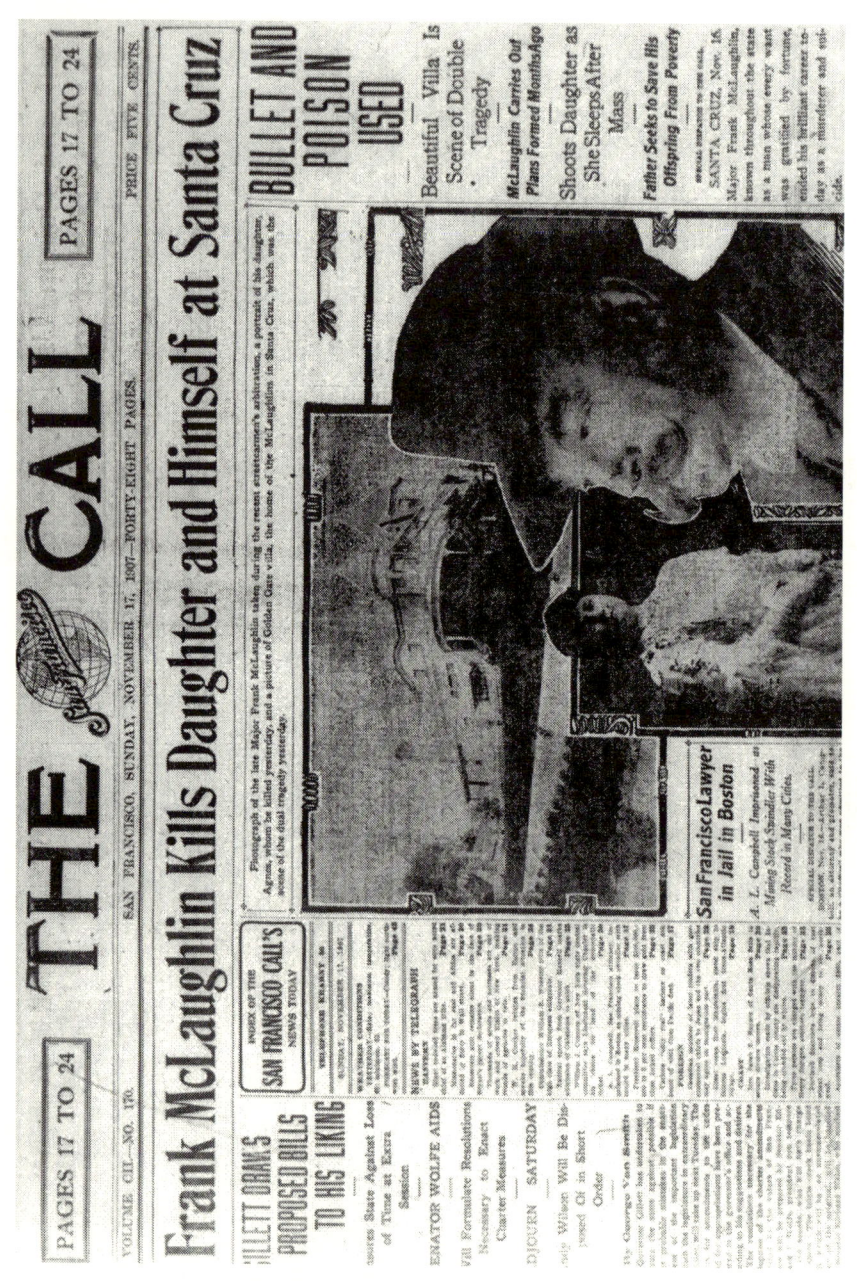

Supernatural Santa Cruz - Second Edition
PART II: Confidential Locations

San Francisco Call article, 1907

Supernatural Santa Cruz - Second Edition
PART II: Confidential Locations

Additional Information:
- An owner named the dearly deceased "Angel Agnes" and believes Agnes is a positive guardian of the home.

The Golden Gate Villa's back door to nowhere, Santa Cruz, CA

Location: A private residence located on 3rd Street, Santa Cruz, CA 95060

Sunshine Villa

The Sunshine Villa, previously the old McCray Hotel, holds plenty of history within its walls and surroundings. Legends say that before the classic Victorian was built on the property in the 1860s, the Ohlone Indians performed sacred rituals there and utilized it as burial grounds. For almost a century, the property was incessantly bought and sold, and was abandoned for almost a decade. Police reports state that while the Sunshine Villa was condemned, it was occupied by drug dealers, homeless people, and cultists. The cultists are said to have held satanic rituals throughout the building. Notorious serial killer Herbert Mullin resided there as well back in the late 1970s, during the peak of his killing spree. Mullin was known to practice satanic rites in the tower above.

Sunshine Villa, Santa Cruz, CA

Supernatural Santa Cruz - Second Edition
PART II: Confidential Locations

It was in the 1960s when the McCray Hotel first opened that claims of ghost sightings began to arise. Since then, it has been said that the property has been haunted by spirits from its dreadful past. Housekeepers and other staff members have reported, "Cold presences, mysterious blue lights and the voice of women calling from the shadows," according to a Metro Santa Cruz article in 1999.

Former employees claim to have been touched by an unseen force while working within this aged structure. Another local claimed that while living at the hotel he would see a blue mist materialize in room number 2. Windows and doors are said to open and close on their own, in addition to unexplainable sounds and footsteps.

A friend of mine once worked at the Villa and encountered a few unexplainable events, such as a light turning on and off on its own when the room was unoccupied, as well as being touched.

"One time I was walking the food cart down to the dementia floor and I felt like something was gently pushing my lower back for a couple seconds. I heard a story about a woman in the dementia ward who had never really spoken before, just moaned, but one night woke up and yelled a man's name, the name of the resident who used to live in that room who had passed away there."

A local psychic feels that the spirit of a woman is trapped in the Sunshine Villa; she was murdered there long ago. The

Supernatural Santa Cruz - Second Edition
PART II: Confidential Locations

sensitive believes that the woman's death was covered up somehow and she is still waiting for someone to help her uncover her murder. Accounts of bloodshed, rituals, séances, and dire karma, appear to create a space for ghosts to occupy.

Sunshine Villa, Santa Cruz, CA

Today the Sunshine Villa still remains on Beach Hill, presently as a retirement home for the living and the dead.

Location: Private residences located at 80 Front Street, Santa Cruz, CA 95060

The Edwards' House

On the Davenport cliffs, overlooking Red, White and Blue Beach, stands a cottage known as "The Edwards' House." The home was built and owned by a sea captain in 1857, who is believed to be the spirit haunting the vicinity today. As soon as the Edwards family moved into this home during the 1950s, they noticed a black rain slicker and hat hanging by the back door that didn't belong to any of them. They later started to see the ghost of a sea captain wearing that exact outfit. This ghost was known to roam the perimeter of Red, White and Blue Beach and was seen by hundreds of people. The Edwards would also see the ghost walking out their back door.

The Edwards' daughters were constantly awakened by something that would viciously shake their beds at night. Their brother didn't believe them, so he traded beds with one of his sisters. The next morning the Edwards' son reported feeling like the bed was shaking and moving so violently he first thought it was an earthquake.

The next horrifying disturbance was when a large, heavy navy picture hanging on the Edwards' wall, was ripped off by an unseen force. The framed photo flew five feet and crashed down into the hardwood floor, embedding glass slivers into the wood. Another uncanny experience occurred in 1975, when owner Kathy Edwards was almost hit by a large potted plant. It flew approximately twelve feet toward her in midair. Luckily, her daughter caught it before it caused Kathy any bodily harm.

One skeptical visitor was laughing about the place being haunted, and within seconds, a drawer near him opened and a baby shoe flew out and hit him on his forehead. Kathy Edwards saw the visitor become a believer after that. Many visitors took the story seriously, including psychic Silvia Browne from Campbell, California. She and other psychics envisioned victims being killed and buried on the property. One psychic said he *saw* a girl named Gwendolyn being murdered there around the turn of the century. Kathy confirmed that this event did in fact occur when she and her husband Ralph dug up a skeleton while putting in a barbeque pit one day. The human remains were examined by an expert, who said the skeleton was from a young woman, buried approximately 70 to 80 years ago.

Doors slamming and footsteps heard throughout the home is nothing compared to what the Edwards family has dealt with. Kathy's perfume bottles were known to clatter around a lot, and many heard sounds of shattering crystal coming from the vicinity as well. Countless amounts of the Edwards' household items were known to disappear and reappear in different locations. Some have even witnessed objects flying through the air. Lights turn on and off after the Edwards are in bed and many campers on the campground complain about the flickering lights that are seen throughout the night on endless occasions.

Supernatural Santa Cruz - Second Edition
PART II: Confidential Locations

Additional Information:
- Witnesses have seen moving blobs and bolts of light, and some have also captured the anomalies on film.

Location: A private residence in Santa Cruz, CA 95060

Supernatural Santa Cruz - Second Edition
PART II: Confidential Locations

Paradise Park

Long ago, Paradise Park was used as a gunpowder facility known as Powder Works, which was shut down shortly after a horrific, accidental explosion that occurred on April 26, 1898. Locals saw sparks in the air and felt a huge blast from two miles away. On that occasion it had killed eleven workers, and over the years, several other explosions had occurred on the land, killing both residents and employees.

Paradise Park, Santa Cruz, CA

The vicinity on and around Paradise Park is claimed to be haunted by past Powder Works employees. Level-headed workers would see ghosts near the location where the former

Supernatural Santa Cruz - Second Edition
PART II: Confidential Locations

employees died. It is said that the ghosts of the former workers are known to make their appearance on the eve of the explosions.

Allegedly, a woman by the name of Lucy Santiago was hit and killed by debris from a Powder Works explosion in 1892, while standing in her doorway, while she was leaving for her wedding. Some claim to see the ghost that perished in the blast, dressed in her wedding gown, walking down Highway 9 late at night; eternally trying to make it to her wedding, which she missed more than 100 years ago.

Paradise Park Entrance, Santa Cruz, CA

Supernatural Santa Cruz - Second Edition
PART II: Confidential Locations

Years later, the site was restored into a private community with a view of the river. In 1997, a couple that had lived there complained about their home being haunted. They alleged that on many occasions they were able to hear voices around the house – voices that spoke a foreign language.

1898 Powder Mill explosion memorial, Santa Cruz Memorial, Santa Cruz, CA

Supernatural Santa Cruz - Second Edition
PART II: Confidential Locations

SANTA CRUZ IN MOURNING FOR ITS DEAD

Bodies of Eleven Victims of the Powder Explosion Recovered.

But Two Are Identified and the Others Will Be Given Public Burial in the Odd Fellows' Cemetery.

THE DEAD.

- James Miller.
- Ernest Marshall.
- Luther Marshall.
- Charles Miller.
- Ernest Jennings.
- Guy Fagen.
- Joe Josephs.
- Charles Cole.
- Henry Butler.
- Ed Gilleran.

The new boiler, which is being put up fifty yards from the scene of the explosion, is the only thing intact.

Across the river every window in the packing houses, and the wheel and press houses is broken, but only one mill is a wreck—that of the refinery, where the saltpeter and soda was mixed.

The scene at the once pretty powder mill village is a sad one. The only structures left standing are the old office, the schoolhouse and several small cottages. The boarding-house is a total wreck.

The fire started from firebrands from the works and commenced at the old lodging-house, where the carpeters roomed. The houses of William Johnson, another lodging-house, the home of Frank Patton, that of John Dennett, George Mower's cottage and the last dwelling on that side of the street, owned by John Welch, went in their turn. The flames then crossed the street and the home of Mrs. J. Rooney was destroyed.

Coroner Clark impaneled the following jury to-day: Henry P. Rice, J.

San Francisco Call article, 1898. Public domain.

Location: Highway 9, Santa Cruz, CA 95060

Supernatural Santa Cruz - Second Edition
PART II: Confidential Locations

The Walnut Street Incubus

According to a Metroactive article in 1999, the ghost of a rapist is said to have once haunted a residence on Walnut Street in downtown Santa Cruz. Allegedly, before he died, the rapist lived in the home and would take advantage of the servant girls who resided there as well. A woman who lived in the house around the 1920s confirmed at least one of the rapes in the front room.

Unaware of the house's uncanny past, five women moved into the home together around 1993. They had to figure out for themselves who else used to occupy the house. In addition the unpleasant residual energy that lingered, three of the women began to have very disturbing and unbelievable experiences in the old dwelling, experiences they would never forget.

One of the victims, Olivia, kept having reoccurring sex dreams and claimed to wake up tired, as if she had just experienced a long night of intercourse. Cynthia, another woman who lived in the home, was able to see the young entity, and claimed that over time it became more volatile. Their housemate, Anna, had also been haunted by the evil entity.

"Now this was a very tough girl. But the minute I asked her, she turned and looked at me and burst into tears. She told me that she'd been having these experiences that when she went to sleep, it felt as if somebody were stroking her hair and touching her body."

Supernatural Santa Cruz - Second Edition
PART II: Confidential Locations

Incubus painting, 1870. Public domain photo.

"We burned some incense in the house and that got rid of him for a while. But then sometime after that, Catherine (another housemate) and I were sitting in kitchen, and no one else was home and we heard this voice say, 'I want you.' It was crystal clear, but at the same time almost like a fading echo. I mean, the hair on our arms stood straight up, and Catherine said, 'Do you think he's back?' We checked inside the house and outside, but nobody else was around," Metroactive article, 1999.

Three days later, Olivia had another dream, ". . . there were all these people out in the backyard dressed in turn-of-the-century farm clothes, knocking on my bedroom window. In my dream I sat up in bed and looked out the window, and they told me, 'You have to wake up because Michael is back.'"

The dilemma became extremely overwhelming and upsetting, especially after two of the women witnessed some dishes in the dish rack being rearranged on their own. They received advice and insight from a psychic who sensed that the rapist once lived in the home with his previous victims. This is when Olivia got into contact with the woman who previously resided there during the 1920s, who knew about a reported raping.

After figuring out who the unpleasant entity was and why he was there, Olivia claimed to speak to him for two weeks, addressing that they are not servants, and that he needs to respect them or leave. She said that the activity completely stopped after her confrontation and they believe that the demonic entity finally went somewhere else.

Location: Walnut Street, Santa Cruz, CA 95060

```
Supernatural Santa Cruz - Second Edition
    PART II: Confidential Locations
```

Supernatural Santa Cruz - Second Edition
PART II: Confidential Locations

ANONYMOUS BUSINESSES

Supernatural Santa Cruz - Second Edition
PART II: Confidential Locations

The Old Santa Cruz Hospital

The Old Santa Cruz Hospital, Santa Cruz, CA, 1950. Public domain photo.

The three-story, aged structure was built in 1929, and was used as the Santa Cruz Hospital, also known as the Sisters' Hospital from 1949 to 1967. Over the years, some have claimed to experience paranormal encounters on the property.

In the early 1990s, a friend of mine claimed to see a white, translucent apparition of a woman float by the front doors of the entryway while standing near the fountain late one evening.

I spoke with another local who said that when he passes the steps of the front entrance, he feels and hears what seems to be

Supernatural Santa Cruz - Second Edition
PART II: Confidential Locations

a crowd of people, although there is no one else in sight. He believes there is a good probability that the hauntings at the plaza have much to do with the fact that it was once a hospital.

The Old Santa Cruz Hospital, Santa Cruz, CA

Location: Santa Cruz, CA 95062

Supernatural Santa Cruz - Second Edition
PART II: Confidential Locations

The Sister Theaters

Two sister theaters in Santa Cruz County are allegedly haunted by both restless and content spirits. Former manager Chet Bauerle, who had paranormal encounters at both venues, gladly shared his other spine-chilling experiences with me.

At the first sister theater, I had heard that the second auditorium was inhabited by a spirit and made guests, as well as workers, feel as if they were being watched. Chet said that he felt the presence I had heard about, and that he doesn't like to be alone in the second auditorium without another worker present. After a midnight showing of *Paranormal Activity 3*, Chet stated that some guests came out of the theater and said, "We don't know what was more scary, the theater or the movie!"

Another eerie incident took place in 2009. One of Chet's coworkers went in to clean Auditorium 2 when he came upon an elderly woman in the theater who was very upset. Apparently, this lady was yelling at him, so he went to find a manager. Within less than a minute, Chet and this staff member came back to the auditorium where the woman had just been, but she was gone. "There is no way she could have gotten out of the auditorium that fast. We checked the back doors; we checked everything, and no sign of the lady."

"Upstairs in the projection booth, I'd go as fast as possible to start movies, thread them up, do whatever I had to do and get out of there. It felt hostility up there, like something didn't want me in there. I was never actually touched, but it was almost like something was pushing you out. As soon as you open the door to the projection booth, you were not welcome."

The third ghost is believed to be the spirit of a former owner, who has been seen walking up the staircase by an employee, and was also sighted in the office by several construction workers. A newer employee told Chet that the spirit of a man kept following him around. After describing his features, Chet concluded that he was being trailed by the old owner. The theater's staff members claim to feel his presence watching over them, and even looking over their shoulder.

Over the years, guests and staff have heard unexplainable sounds in the second sister theater, in addition to feeling as if they are being watched by an invisible force. One night, while my friend was in the Ladies' Room, she felt as if someone was looking at her over the stall in the bathroom.

Right after her unsettling experience, she asked an employee at the concession stand, "Is this place haunted?" The employee believed it was, and said that she also had something strange happen to her in a bathroom stall.

Chet Bauerle had several unexplained encounters, particularly during the late hours of the night and after closing. "As closing manager, when you were there alone or with one other person, you always feel as if you're being watched, or that something was trying to help you. It wasn't necessarily friendly, but it also wasn't necessarily hostel. There are about five areas of the building that just feel off."

Chet's most eerie encounter took place in Auditorium 1, while previewing movies after hours. While he was watching a film, he saw curtains near the exit sign begin to move. "The curtains would slightly move back and you'd see this figure look out," Chet explained. He said the ghost looked like an ethnic homeless person and wonders if maybe someone had gotten trapped and died in the vicinity long ago. His friend had also witnessed the figure standing near the exit on a different occasion, in addition to feeling the unsettling presence that lingers when the theater is practically empty. "I never went back into that auditorium unless there were other people in there," he stated.

Additional Information:
- Chet once saw the dark figure of a male standing in the hallway near Auditorium 3 after hours one night. It was there for only a second before it disappeared.

PART III:
Cryptozoology Creatures

```
Supernatural Santa Cruz - Second Edition
PART III: Cryptozoology Creatures
```

Supernatural Santa Cruz - Second Edition
PART III: Cryptozoology Creatures

Bigfoot in Santa Cruz County

Deep in the Santa Cruz Mountains sits The Bigfoot Discovery Museum, owned by Michael Rugg and Paula Yarr. As a child, Michael witnessed a Bigfoot while camping in Garberville, California. For more than fifty years he has researched, investigated, and searched for the proof of Sasquatch.

The Bigfoot Discovery Museum, Felton, CA

Supernatural Santa Cruz - Second Edition
PART III: Cryptozoology Creatures

The Bigfoot Museum opened in 1998. As soon as it did, local witnesses started coming in to talk about their experiences with the Bigfoot around the Santa Cruz Mountains. Several have said they heard large, heavy footsteps and breathing on their porches at night. One local from Felton in particular couldn't wait to share his story with Rugg. Earlier that year, he claimed to see a Sasquatch walking across a ridge behind his home near the Zyante Creek during broad daylight.

The Bigfoot Discovery Project is run with the help of paranormal enthusiast and Sasquatch hunter, Ralph Jack. Ralph has been interested in Bigfoot for decades and has had encounters with the beast as well. In 2011, while hunting for a Yeti late in the night in Big Basin, Mike and Ralph recorded at least four loud calls from anomalies, and received other vocalizations as well. One scream lasted up to fifty seconds.

In 2003, other eye witnesses reported seeing Bigfoot in their back yard one night, after hearing loud footsteps, grunting sounds, and their pet chicken cackle from across their back porch. When they went out back to investigate the uncanny sounds, they saw a large dark figure leap over their six-foot gate and run off into the woods. The next morning, Michael Rugg came to check out the scene in Ben Lomond. Right behind the gate there was a trail of plucked chicken feathers leading down further into the wilderness. Rugg followed the trail and it lead him to the chicken that had been stolen and killed the night before. They wondered why something would just hunt for their food and then leave it. The owners then recalled turning on their backyard lights after the incident, which probably scared the monster away.

Another encounter scared the daylights out of a Boulder Creek local, who was hanging out in his hot tub around 2 am one night. The victim was just relaxing when he heard and felt a huge banging coming from underneath the hot tub, shaking it and the deck it sat on. The Boulder Creek local jumped out of his hot tub and ran into his house. The next day he went to investigate what he had experienced the night before. Below the tall deck was something the local had never seen before. A pair of plastic karate nunchucks were placed neatly right below where the local had been sitting in his hot tub the night before. He felt as if the child's toy was deliberately placed there for him. The local decided to go ask his next door neighbor if she had any idea whose they were. Surprisingly they belonged to his neighbor's son, who had lost the nunchucks in the woods about ten to eleven years ago. It is believed by many that Bigfoot is known to bring gifts to people. Rugg and the victim hypothesized that the hairy beast needed to get the local's attention so that he would find his prize.

Along with hearing about local sightings from Rugg at the museum, you can observe the large map on their wall with dozens of thumb tacks showing where Bigfoot has been sighted in our county. Rugg has several recordings of unexplainable howls in the night and sounds of heavy tree branches smacking each other. Many researchers believe that's how the Sasquatches communicate with one another.

Rugg once found a big tooth and showed it to five dentists on separate occasions. They all concluded that "the tooth looked just like a human's upper molar, but was way too big."

The Museum also has numerous foot casts of Sasquatch from various locations over the years. The Bigfoot Discovery Museum provides lots of photos and tons of memorabilia of the legendary Bigfoot, as well as showing the famous Patterson-Gimlin film that's played at the museum throughout the day. In 1967, the Patterson film was recorded by Roger Patterson in Bluff Creek. There, Roger filmed a Bigfoot walking along the creek into the woods.

I find one of the most popular questions skeptics say is "Well, if there *is* such thing as Bigfoot, why hasn't anyone found a body?" There are a few alleged reasons that a Bigfoot corpse has never been found. Rugg pointed out that, statistically, when an animal dies in the woods, its body can be completely gone and eaten by other animals within five to seven days. Unless there are hikers hiking out in the deep woods around the time the Bigfoot had died, the chances of finding a corpse or remains (of any animal really) isn't very likely. Some researchers believe that Bigfoot lives underground and stays there the majority of the time, so they would most likely die underground, where no one would ever discover a body. Some also believe that Sasquatches bury their dead.

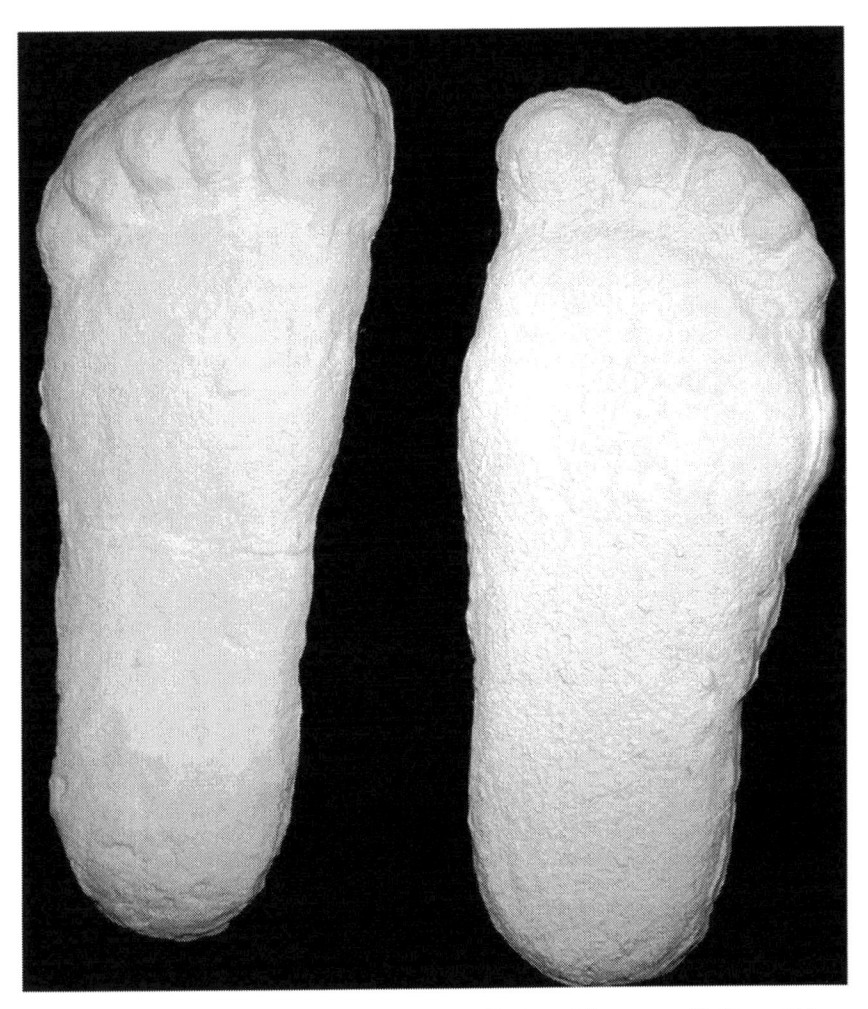

Supernatural Santa Cruz - Second Edition
PART III: Cryptozoology Creatures

Patterson-Gimlin Sasquach casts, Bigfoot Museum, Felton, CA

Supernatural Santa Cruz - Second Edition
PART III: Cryptozoology Creatures

Owner Michael Rugg with Assistant, Ralph Jack, Bigfoot Museum, Felton, CA

Bigfoot has been seen, investigated, and talked about for hundreds of years. The Ohlone Indians called Bigfoot "Chuntana" and would warn the Indian children to stay close to their campsite at night or the "Chuntana" would get them. There are theories that Bigfoot and aliens are linked and that Bigfoot may even be from outer space. Dozens of people from around the US have sighted a Bigfoot and a UFO near each other, or in the same vicinity as one another.

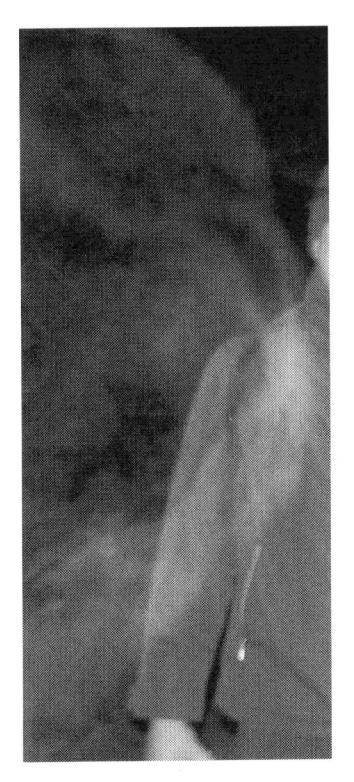

Supernatural Santa Cruz - Second Edition
PART III: Cryptozoology Creatures

Possible baby Bigfoot apparition, Felton, CA, photo by Michael Rugg

Additional Information:

- There have been reports of more than 160 experiences with Bigfoot in the Santa Cruz Mountains.

- In 2012, a Bigfoot was sighted and heard near Quail Hollow, Ben Lomond, California, by two different individuals within two weeks of each other.

Location: Santa Cruz County, CA

Supernatural Santa Cruz - Second Edition
PART III: Cryptozoology Creatures

The Sea Monster of Monterey Bay

A sea monster by the name of "Old Man of Monterey Bay" has been sighted on several occasions, with reports dating as far back as the 1920s, regarding a creature that's about 30 to 40 feet long that swims right below the surface of the ocean. In 1922, a fisherman was sailing home when he saw something bobbing up and down in the ocean about a half a mile away. Worried that it might be someone in danger he sped over to it. Within about 100 feet, he noticed it wasn't human, but a sea monster. The Captain described the creature to have a head the size of a 50-gallon drum and its forehead was huge and protruding. Standing there staring at the monster's unearthly face, the fisherman recalled that there had just been reports of two fishermen who had vanished while at sea. Quickly, he turned on the boat's engine and headed back home, deciding that he wouldn't tell anyone about the incident.

The Captain had his second sighting in Half Moon Bay, 16 years after his first. This time he was accompanied by his brother-in-law and his crew. His brother-in-law began telling stories to the captain of a creature he saw a few times near the Monterey Submarine Canyon. Coincidentally, the monster swam up to the boat soon after he had told his story. The captain called out for all hands on deck. The crew all saw what the captain had witnessed before. The cook exclaimed, "It has the face of a monkey. Let's leave. This place is a bad omen." (As stated in Monterey Weekly Article 2007) The Captain's brother-in-law argued that he thought the sea monster's face looked more like an old man's. The crew described the sea monster to be about as long as their 45 foot ship and was very large and brown with extremely saggy and wrinkly skin. "The Old Man of Monterey Bay" slowly sank down under the water while the crew kept arguing on what the sea monster looked like.

In 1925, a creature which is believed to be a plesiosaurus by several scientists, washed up on the shore two miles north of Santa Cruz. Many locals and researchers believe that this sea creature is what had been spotted for the last few years, and that the Plesiosaurus is the "Old Man of Monterey Bay." But wait. How are they even comparable? A Plesiosaurus' face looks similar to a dolphin's face. The sea monster that was witnessed swimming near the fishermans' boats had the face of a "monkey" or an "old man."

The sea monster was sighted by many other fishermen over the years and was referred to by some as "Bobo – The Old Man of the Sea." Bobo was sighted in 1940 near the Monterey Trench by another captain and his crew. In the late 1940s, a sudden increase in sightings was reported near Monterey, Pacific Grove, and Fort Ord.

In 1948, The Old Man of the Sea was sighted by nine crew members on the Monterey Trench. The crew members observed the sea creature's long neck six feet above the water line. They said the monster looked humanoid and "had a flat nose and large blinking eyes," according to the book *Supernatural California*.

Bobo was never reported after 1948. Although rumors still flock the town that some fisherman do spot the sea monster, but are just reluctant to report it because doing so could harm their reputations.

Additional Information:
- There have been several reports of the Sea Monster spotted south of the wharf over the years.

Location: Monterey Bay, CA

PART IV:

Surrounding Areas

Supernatural Santa Cruz - Second Edition
PART IV: Surrounding Areas

Pacheco Pass

Over the centuries, numerous deaths have occurred on and around "Blood Alley" creating its dark history. It is alleged that Indians were massacred by where the highway now lies. This, along with many other events and accidents that have occurred at or around this site, is believed to have created a residual energy to forever repeat itself. Some claim that "it's almost a Bermuda Triangle on land," quoted from the book *Supernatural California*. People have claimed to see ghosts that are dressed as if they lived as far back as the 1700s. There have been reports of Indians, soldiers, and settlers on wagons witnessed along Pacheco Pass. Many people have seen a man believed to be a Franciscan Monk, describing him as wearing a black robe and standing on the side of the road between Casa De Fruta and Bell's Station. Others have reported seeing a headless man walking on the side of Pacheco Pass near Bolsa Road.

Witnesses claim to have seen a hitchhiking ghost around the area. The young girl, seen dressed in jeans and a plaid shirt, who now haunts the vicinity, was tragically hit by a semi-truck while trying to hitch a ride long ago. It is alleged by various truck drivers that they've pulled over to give the phantom hitchhiker a ride, and have even spoken with the ghost, whom they believed to be alive at the time. As she would walk around the truck to the passenger door, she would suddenly vanish.

Supernatural Santa Cruz - Second Edition
PART IV: Surrounding Areas

In a small grove of rocks off the highway near the mission, the ghost of a woman has been seen on occasion late at night. She appears in her wedding dress in the vicinity where her fiancé allegedly died in a car wreck. After his death, the ghost bride took her life by jumping off the rocks, hoping to join her love once again.

Pacheco Pass can be upsetting or frightening to some sensitives or psychics. Sylvia Browne is one such person. Browne claimed to receive psychic images there, and said she saw "a little girl in a covered wagon cowering with her fists pressed against her eyes while Indians raged around the wagon train. Her sense of hopelessness was overwhelming," quoted from *Haunted Houses of California*.

Additional Information:
- The ghost of a woman in a Victorian dress has been sighted along the road. It is alleged that she's endlessly searching for her child.

Location: Highway 152, (The highway connecting Watsonville and Gilroy, CA)

The Monterey Hotel

Built in 1904, the historic, elegant, and beautiful Monterey Hotel in downtown Monterey has been claimed to be haunted for decades. The hotel's most well-known ghost, Fred (the past maintenance man), died when he was crushed in the elevator shaft, which is no longer used, and where high EMF is also found. Fred lived in Room 217 for years, and it is believed by many that he still does. To this day, he definitely makes an effort to make people acknowledge his existence. Guests and employees have alleged seeing objects move on their own in Room 217, such as a TV sliding out from a hutch, and the wooden blinds have been witnessed moving when the windows are closed. Strange, uncanny popping sounds have been heard in the hotel room, along with disembodied voices.

The ghost of a little girl has also been witnessed running past, and standing in front of Room 217. Visitors have claimed to hear a child running past the door in the middle of the night. Some claim to hear knocking at their door and find no one there when they answer it. Legend has it that the little girl and her sister were murdered by their mother in Room 407. Occasionally, the little girl has also been witnessed standing at the top of the stairs that look down upon the lobby during the wee hours of the night. A couple of psychics claim that the little girl is scared of some of the hotel's male employees for some reason.

The majority of the employees believe that the hotel is severely haunted. Fady, the hotel manager, claims that *Do Not Disturb* signs are randomly moved from door to door, and this is believed to be caused by the little girl. Fady has encountered papers on the front desk being moved and shuffled around many times when no one else was around. He has also seen something in the office closing the heavy door, which had a door stop in front of it. He said that if a glass of water is left out, that it will be emptied, sometimes within minutes.

Chris, a Monterey Hotel employee, also encountered the office door closing on him, as well as the radio (with a solid button) turning on by itself. He has noticed an unexplainable hot spot, only recognized at times behind the front desk. He said that the temperature difference is very noticeable and that he can feel the temperature drop while he's standing only a foot away from the warm area. Lights have been said to turn on and off on their own, and mysterious whispers have been heard throughout the hotel.

Ahmed, another staff member, has heard disembodied voices pass him while walking the halls. Once he heard a ghost mimic his voice over the walkie-talkie. He also had an unexplainable encounter when he saw something moving on its own, along with an apparition that looked right at him. His friend quit his very first night working at the Monterey Hotel when he looked up to see the ghost of a man standing at the front desk.

In 2011, a hotel security guard was actually lifted up by a spirit while sitting in her chair in the area of the building that is being remodeled. She felt the entity lift her several inches off the ground, holding her up for a few seconds before placing her back in her seat.

The basement is believed to have the most paranormal activity in the hotel. Two construction workers quit on the spot after they were both scratched by an unseen force while down in the basement. Two employees saw the scratch marks and their only explanation was that it was caused by something paranormal.

Supernatural Santa Cruz - Second Edition
PART IV: Surrounding Areas

Additional Information:

- A lady in white has been witnessed by individuals in the hotel's breakfast room.

- The apparition of a man dressed in Edwardian clothing and a top hat has been seen in the mirror located in the lobby.

- The ghost of a Hispanic female housekeeper has been seen on the top floors of the hotel. Some people don't even realize that she is a phantom until she vanishes without a trace.

Location: 406 Alvarado Street, Monterey, CA 93940
(831) 375-3184
www.montereyhotel.com

Supernatural Santa Cruz - Second Edition
PART IV: Surrounding Areas

The Winchester Mystery House

The enchanting Winchester Mystery House was built around the clock from 1884 to 1922. The gothic Victorian was owned, designed, and occupied by Sarah Winchester, wife of William Winchester, whose father invented the famous Winchester rifle.

Sarah and William were married in 1862 and conceived a child four years later. In 1866, their infant, Annie, died of a rare disease. Fifteen years later, William Winchester died of Tuberculosis. Both of these deaths were traumatizing for Sarah; she lived the rest of her life in mourning.

Sarah Winchester was always very interested in the paranormal, and decided to see a psychic to help with her grief. Sarah met with a medium from Boston who told her she was being haunted by the Indians who were killed from the rifles her father-in-law and husband produced. The psychic also explained that the spirits caused her husband's and daughter's untimely deaths, and that she could be next. To save herself, the medium told Sarah to build a house out west for the Indian spirits to reside. Trusting the psychic, whom she just had met, Sarah quickly bought an 8-bedroom home in Santa Clara Valley. She immediately hired carpenters to work nonstop to add more rooms to the house. In the end, it was transformed into a seven-story mansion containing 160 rooms, 2,000 doors, 10,000 windows, 47 stairways, 47 fireplaces, thirteen bathrooms and six kitchens.

Supernatural Santa Cruz – Second Edition
PART IV: Surrounding Areas

What made the mansion even more unique was that Sarah Winchester had the carpenters build doors to nowhere and staircases that lead to ceilings. She believed that these bizarre passageways would confound the evil spirits, in hopes that they would leave in confusion.

Every night until her death, Sarah communicated with the spirits in her séance room known as the "The Blue Room." At midnight, she'd ring the bell in the tower to summon the spirits, and then she'd speak with them using the automatic writing method. During that time, Sarah received messages from the spirits, instructing her to proceed with the construction of the home. At 2 am, she'd ring the bell again to close the nightly channeling.

The number thirteen was very intriguing to Sarah Winchester. Believing that it signified good luck, she ordered parts of the property to be decorated and constructed in multiples of thirteen. Sarah had her driveway lined with thirteen palm trees, had thirteen bathrooms built in the house, many ceilings had thirteen panels, and rooms had thirteen windows. She wore thirteen robes during her séances, signed her will thirteen times and even detailed the mansion with Chandeliers that had thirteen lights, thirteen hooks, thirteen drainage holes in a few sinks, and thirteen daisies (her favorite flower) in various stained glass windows.

Sarah would sometimes find bizarre traces of signs from the spirits, and she took their warnings very seriously. One night,

Supernatural Santa Cruz - Second Edition
PART IV: Surrounding Areas

Sarah Winchester went down to her wine cellar and discovered a black handprint on the wall. The spirits told her later that it was a print from a demon's hand. Sarah was horrified and believed it was a word of warning to not drink alcohol. She immediately had the cellar sealed off with all her bottles of liquor still stocked and to this day it has never been located.

Sarah Winchester passed away while sleeping in her bed on September 5, 1922. After her death, it was believed by many that her spirit roamed the haunted halls of the sprawling mansion. Some people have actually caught a glimpse of Sarah Winchester at the Mystery House. Ghost Hunter and writer Antoinette May investigated the Winchester Mystery House with well-known psychic Sylvia Browne. In May's book titled *Haunted Houses and Wandering Ghosts of California*, she writes, "While sitting in Sarah Winchester's bedroom, Sylvia and I saw great balls of red light that seemed to explode before us."

Over the years, dozens of people have reported having paranormal experiences on the property, such as hearing footsteps, chains rattling, whispers, organ music playing, hammering, and feeling breezes and cold spots. There have been reports of smelling food cooking as well. Orbs are seen on the property, along with shadows, mystical lights, apparitions, and door knobs turning on their own.

Several people believe that ghosts of old employees roam the property. One ghost in particular has been seen on many occasions in the basement, dressed in white overalls, sometimes pushing a wheelbarrow. The ghost has also been witnessed walking up the stairs to the mansion, and then suddenly vanishing.

Annette Martin, who passed away recently in 2011, was a psychic from Los Gatos who claimed to have conversed with a spirit named Clyde on several occasions, who is also said to haunt the Winchester Mystery House. Allegedly, Clyde told the psychic that he had been a groundskeeper for Sarah Winchester, and had promised to look over the property for eternity. Annette claimed that the ghost would meet her at the front entrance whenever she came to visit, concerned with the crowds of people going in and out of his boss's home.

Location: 525 South Winchester Boulevard, San Jose, CA 95124

(408) 247-2000

www.winchestermysteryhouse.com

Supernatural Santa Cruz - Second Edition
PART IV: Surrounding Areas

The Golden Gate Bridge

Built in 1937, The Golden Gate Bridge is known for being the most popular suicide location in the world. Since the bridge opened, over 1,300 people have jumped to their deaths, falling 4,200 feet into the sea. It is claimed that on foggy nights you can hear the quiet screams of the people who fell into the darkness. Several people have claimed to have observed ghosts and apparitions on the bridge shrouded by the fog. They say they stand on the edge of the bridge and then suddenly disappear seconds to a minute later.

In 1853, a ship known as the SS Tennessee vanished in the strait, near where the bridge was later built. Since its unexplainable disappearance, the ship has been seen by countless people over the years. Some have said to have sighted the phantom ship pass below the bridge and disappear minutes later. In 1942, a crew member aboard the USS Kennison saw the late SS Tennessee's ghostly apparition pass by. After watching the eerie vessel fade away into the night, he noticed that it did not register on his ship's radar.

Location: The Bridge that connects San Francisco Bay and Marin County, CA

Supernatural Santa Cruz - Second Edition
PART IV: Surrounding Areas

Alcatraz

Before Alcatraz was used as a prison, it was occupied by the Ohlone Indians. The Ohlones believed that the island was cursed by evil spirits who inhabited the area. The Indians also used the island as a place for criminals to reside. Over the years, many people died on this twenty-two-acre land mass known as "The Rock," it stands a mile and a half off the shore of San Francisco. In addition to all of the Indians who are said to have died on The Rock, many inmates passed away during their stay at the penitentiary.

Records indicate that eight people were murdered by inmates and five prisoners committed suicide. Fifteen died from natural illnesses, and seven were shot and killed while trying to escape. Two prisoners drowned and five others vanished, and are still unaccounted for. Being that this is one of the strictest and most uncomfortable state prisons, as well as with all of the deaths, anger, rage and despair that occurred over the years, there is no doubt that Alcatraz is inhabited by ghosts.

The most common paranormal activity that occurs in this penitentiary is unexplainable sounds. Footsteps are heard throughout the halls, as well as disembodied voices. Security guards and other employees have claimed to hear ghostly moaning or crying, along with men's uncanny voices, whistles, and screams. Many people say that they have heard a banjo being played in the shower room. It is believed that the music is played by the ghost of the legendary Al Capone.

Part of Alcatraz has an area where the prisoners were confined inside a steel box in complete darkness for days to weeks at a time. The incarceration boxes are known as the "holes," and are believed to be haunted. Cell block 14D is allegedly haunted by a supernatural creature with red glowing eyes. Since the 1940s, there have been claims of this eerie being sighted there. The sounds of screaming have been heard from the hole, and many people claim that this particular cell is always freezing-cold, even if the next cell over is warm.

People have claimed to see dark shadows move around the building at night. Others have said to have witnessed full-body apparitions. While performing a head count, two security guards claimed to have seen the face of the old convict who mysteriously died in 14D years ago. As soon as they recognized the deceased prisoner, he vanished. EVPs have been caught over the years at Alcatraz. When the famous team TAPS from the show *Ghost Hunters* investigated the island, they picked up an EVP from a former inmate. When they asked whom they were speaking with, they heard a disembodied voice over the recorder say "Harry Brunette, 374." Harry Brunette was a former inmate that stayed at Alcatraz for many years.

Psychic Sylvia Browne held a séance in the dining room after identifying the spirit of a convict by the name of Abie Maldowitz, also known as "Butcher." Sylvia was able to see the ghost

Supernatural Santa Cruz - Second Edition
PART IV: Surrounding Areas

visually and encouraged him to go into the light and cross over, but he was in disbelief that such a place existed. The spirit of Butcher is still known to haunt the penitentiary, particularly in the laundry room where he was murdered.

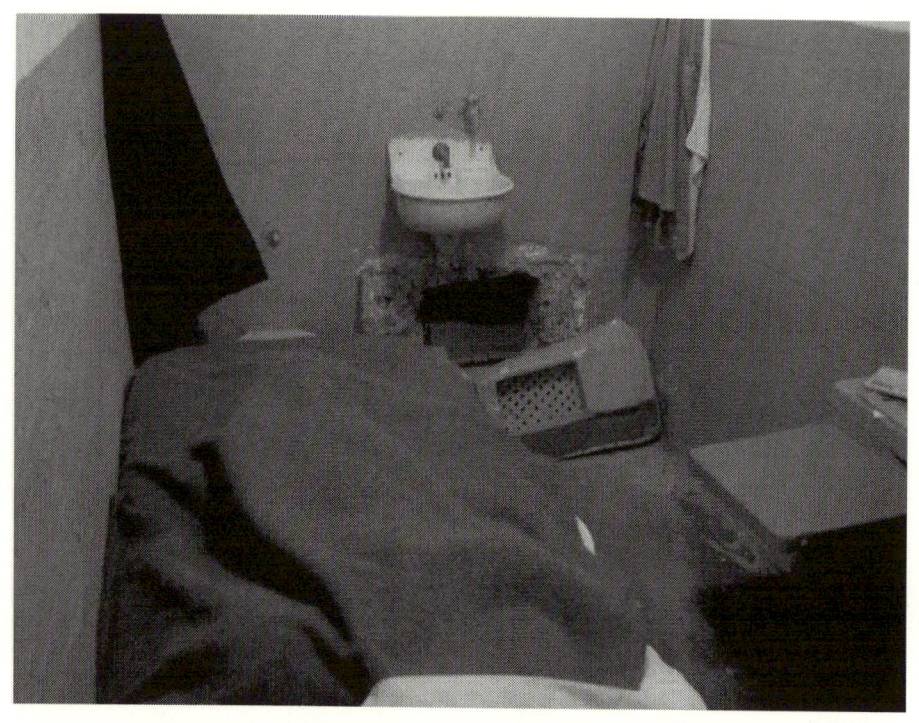

An Alcatraz prison cell with a chiseled air vent made by one of the prisoners, who attempted to escape, courtesy of Wikipedia

Location: Alcatraz Island, San Francisco, CA 94133

PART V:
Miscellaneous and Mystic Enchantment

```
Supernatural Santa Cruz - Second Edition
PART V: Miscellaneous and Mystic Enchantment
```

Supernatural Santa Cruz - Second Edition
PART V: Miscellaneous and Mystic Enchantment

The Virgin Mary Tree

Supernatural Santa Cruz - Second Edition
PART V: Miscellaneous and Mystic Enchantment

Since 1993, thousands of people have visited what is believed as a Virgin Mary tree. On June 17, 1993, a Hispanic woman by the name of Anita Contreras was praying for her child underneath a shady oak tree on the edge of Pinto Lake in Watsonville, California. To her amazement, when Anita looked up, she saw what she believed to be the outline of the Virgin Mary on a large branch.

Soon after she discovered the spiritual image, the word got out quickly, and several people started visiting the tree daily. A massive shrine with statues, pictures, drawings, paintings, lit candles, human hair, trinkets, and literally hundreds of fresh bouquets of flowers surround this mystical tree.

Part of the Virgin Mary tree shrine, Pinto Lake County Park, Watsonville, CA

Supernatural Santa Cruz - Second Edition
PART V: Miscellaneous and Mystic Enchantment

Many people come to pray and worship at the site regularly, even to this day. I spoke with a Pinot Lake staff member who said his friend's mother is a true believer and prays at the site almost weekly.

Virgin Mary tree shrine, Pinto Lake County Park, Watsonville, CA

Sensitives may be able to feel the strong emotional residue in the vicinity due to the belief, commitment, and faith in the tree.

Years back, while celebrating mass at the sacred site, Father Roman Bunda stated, "For those who believe, no explanation is necessary. For those who don't believe, no explanation is possible."

Location: Pinto Lake County Park, Watsonville, CA

Supernatural Santa Cruz - Second Edition
PART V: Miscellaneous and Mystic Enchantment

The Sycamore Grove Spider

One of the oldest tall tales of Santa Cruz was first told by the Ohlone Indian tribe, who believed that the flat area from Highway 9 to the San Lorenzo River was cursed. The story is that a giant supernatural spider inhabited the dark and uncanny grove, feeding off of humans, humans with bad intentions.

The Ohlone Indians claimed that the people who hid darkness in their souls and passed by the area would get tangled in the mystical spider's web and be trapped for all eternity. Some tribe members said they saw the enormous web, "jeweled by dew drops from the fog, deep in the woods." Witnesses reported seeing stolen souls wander the area. This legend carried throughout history, and is still told by a few locals today, who say that spirits killed by the supernatural spider still haunt the Sycamore Grove.

Location: Off Highway 9, Pogonip area, Santa Cruz, CA 95060

The Ohlone Indians

Ohlone Indians dressed up for an event, 1806, drawing by unknown, public domain photo

The Ohlone Indians settled on California's central coast in 10,000 B.C.E. The local tribe, known as the Awaswas, was known to live throughout Santa Cruz County and spoke a variety of different languages. The Ohlones, also known as Costanoans, were very spiritual, and had several supernatural and mythological stories that they told. Unfortunately, the majority of the tales were lost over time, and only a few remain, such as the story of the Sycamore Grove Spider or the Chuntana legends. (For more information, please see Sycamore Grove Spider and Bigfoot in Santa Cruz County stories.)

Supernatural Santa Cruz - Second Edition
PART V: Miscellaneous and Mystic Enchantment

Sacred Indian burial grounds are still being discovered around the county. The most well-known burial sites are found along Beach Hill and the area near Pogonip. In August of 2011, a company bought a lot of land to build apartment buildings at the end of Market and Isabel Drive in Santa Cruz. While excavating the property, 6,000-year-old remains of a young boy and an adult were found. Still planning to build on the site, locals went on strike to try and preserve the sacred, historic land.

"Haven't they seen the movie *Poltergeist?*" A neighbor exclaimed.

Another local stated, "My mother believed that when a burial site is disturbed, the spirit of the individual is wandering," Santa Cruz Patch Article, September 19, 2011.

Hearing the locals' concerns and wishes, the company still proceeds with the project, but will build a sacred site on the land called The Knoll. It will be fenced off and contain the Indian remains that were found, although I and many others believe that the property shouldn't have been touched in the first place.

Spirits of the Awaswas tribe have been heard and sighted throughout Santa Cruz County. Mission Santa Cruz has several of their spirits lingering. The sound of drumming coming from the mission was recorded by a friend and I in 2011. Pogonip Park is also said to be inhabited by the spirits of Indians, and burdened by an old Ohlone curse. (See Pogonip story.)

Supernatural Santa Cruz - Second Edition
PART V: Miscellaneous and Mystic Enchantment

Ghosts of the Indians have been seen by commuters along scenic roads during the hours of darkness.

On Highway 17, as well as on Lee Road in Watsonville, the spirit of an old Indian man has been sighted traveling on foot.

Supernatural Santa Cruz - Second Edition
PART V: Miscellaneous and Mystic Enchantment

Santa Cruz Psychics

LeAndra Johnson

Psychic, Medium, Reiki Master, and Ayurvedic practitioner LeAndra Johnson has been receiving messages from the dead all her life, and has helped hundreds of people, emotionally and physically, since she was very young.

LeAndra provides several services such as Psychic readings, channeling, Light work, Reiki healing and teaching, as well as

Supernatural Santa Cruz - Second Edition
PART V: Miscellaneous and Mystic Enchantment

Ayurveda counseling at her office on the west side of Santa Cruz. "I didn't choose this line of work; it chose me," says LeAndra.

I received Reiki treatment from LeAndra when I injured my back and was bed ridden in 2010. Before I saw her, I couldn't sit down, and could barely even bend my body. After only three Reiki sessions with LeAndra, I felt very close to back to normal again.

While LeAndra gave me readings, she informed me of certain things in great detail that may happen in my future; so far they've all come to pass.

"What is your insight on life after death?" I asked.

"Life doesn't end when the heart stops beating. The one thing I can say I have learned is that just because you go to the other side, it doesn't mean that you know all the answers, because you don't. You are where you left off and are still learning, just at a different level. You're going to come back where you left off. Sometimes I've had to tell that to people that who were contemplating taking their own lives. I told them that one of the things they need to consider is that they will escape this particular body, but not the feeling, and their spirit will remain the same," LeAndra replied.

"Has anyone ever asked you to channel a loved one, and you were unable to because they had reincarnated?" I asked.

"You know that actually has happened to me. It only happened once, but it did happen. I wasn't able to figure it out at first," answered LeAndra.

"So everyone's different right? Some people could die, cross over, and be a spirit for 300 years and then reincarnate? And then some people could die and reincarnate right away?" I asked.

"Yeah," LeAndra replied. "I'm not sure how the time frame works for everybody . . . but yeah."

Contact Information:
Ancient Wisdom Healing Services
402 Ingalls Street, Suite 10
Santa Cruz, CA 95060
www.ancientwisdomhealingservices.com

Tai Miller

The local Santa Cruz Psychic and Medium has been receiving messages from the beyond since as far back as she can remember. Tai recently became an employed psychic in the beginning of 2012. She helps earth-bound spirits cross over and provides Tarot readings, Psychic readings, and channeling as well.

The first paranormal encounter that Tai can remember clearly really frightened her; she was thirteen, staying with her family in a hotel for a couple of weeks. "I saw a dead guy on the ground between our beds in our hotel room and I jumped up and I ran into the living room and said 'Oh my God, there's a dead guy on the bed!'" Tai's parents told her she must have been dreaming, but she knew what she saw, and she felt that the man had died due to a drug overdose in the room. Tai's step brother was said to have sighted the ghost of the man as well. "So the next day I went to the hotel office window and asked if anyone had died in my room. The woman told me that they weren't supposed to talk about it and slammed the window shut. So I thought, Okay – I guess I wasn't just dreaming," Tai said.

"Do you know if the majority of people have two spirit guides, or is it all just completely different?" I asked.

"I think it's completely different. I think some people need more, or they might be someone like you, who's really shiny and attracts spirits. And then there are also people like me who practice communicating with spirits, and therefore collect more spirit guides," Tai replied.

"How did you find out you had a gift to help people? Was there a certain moment or occasion?" I asked.

"There was a certain occasion, actually. I didn't know it for a long time, but when ghosts would show up, I'd move them over. Sometimes I'm not even aware of it. Sometimes just my mere presence is enough," Tai stated.

She came to realize she did have a special gift that was imperative and needed after her co-worker died years back when he was hit by a truck.

"It just knocked him out of his body so quickly, that he didn't know he was dead," Tai said.

He still went to work every day unaware that it was time to move on, and that his soul no longer inhabited his body.

"It was the first time I just really heard someone talking in my head, like a real conversation. I was getting more advanced in the practice and could hear him in a wave," Tai continued.

Tai heard her deceased co-worker say, "Something must be wrong. Why are my parents here?"

As soon as she explained he was dead, Tai and everyone in the room felt him cross over.

"So, I was thinking, I wonder if I could do that deliberately, and everything in me just said, 'Yes, you are supposed to be helping dead people and that is what you are supposed to be doing with this talent,'" Tai exclaimed.

Contact Information:
Caledonia's Psychic Services
(831) 421-9942
taiette.miller@gmail.com
www.caledoniapsychic.com

Shelly Crowley

Psychic Shelly Crowley with author, Aubrey Graves, 2013

The Boulder Creek sensitive and healer was born seeing emotions as colors around people, as well as around some objects.

"My mother told me to not let others know what I can see or what I can do – I would not fit in. She too had gifts, although not as strong as mine. I was nine years old when I figured out that others really don't see them.

"I can visibly see love; it is a golden rope or thread between two souls. It is like gold or mercury and sometimes can glitter if it is new or hopeful love. Sadness presents itself in colors of a muted waterfall, with an iridescent sheen. The colors run like a watercolor, dripping in extreme distress."

Not only is Shelly capable of observing colors of emotion, she is also able to see spirits, in addition to possessing the gift to heal people. She explained to me that spirits look just like normal, living people to her . . . except that they don't have feet and never look straight into her eyes. She observes them all over town and says that Santa Cruz County is filled with them – particularly the spirits of old hippies from the '60s and of animals.

At a young age, the psychic began to notice that she was capable of healing animals by placing both of her hands on or over the injury, helping to relieve and/or take the pain away. Over the years, Shelly's gift has become more known around town. Since 2009, she has been helping about thirty people per week, reducing their pain. Whether it is a tooth ache or a sprained ankle, she never charges for her services.

Contact Information:
Shelly Crowley
P.O. Box 1596
Boulder Creek, CA 95006

Life as a Conduit

Being a conduit, especially in Santa Cruz where the veils are exceptionally thin, is definitely a challenge. For the majority of my life, I had no idea that my energy actually attracted spirits to the point where they visit me regularly, attaching themselves to me. I knew I was sensitive, but was unaware that so much of my anxiety was created by the many ghosts hanging around constantly. I became conscious of my gift when I began communicating with the departed, becoming more open with them. In 2011, about seven months after I first started writing about the paranormal and ghost hunting, my husband and I moved near Santa Cruz Memorial, where things really started to get weird.

After of a number of unexplainable and uncanny events began to occur in our home, I decided to get insight from several different psychics. Within the year, I have spoken with six sensitives, who all believe I am a major conduit, and living near a cemetery really doesn't help. Two of the psychics could actually *see* spirits walking up our street and driveway at night to visit me. Two others could feel it and they said that they felt like our home was a revolving door. It shocked me, but at the same time I felt like it made sense. I knew this was something I needed to be aware of and that I will have to deal with for the rest of my life. At times, ghosts give me so much anxiety that it almost masks everything about them. I don't know if I'm subconsciously protecting myself, or if my spirit guides are protecting me, but it's much harder for me to tune into the spirits that are haunting me than it is to tune into others. That is pretty typical, though. Writing about the paranormal also feels inviting to them, I think. Sometimes I'll have to stop working on a book for a while if the house gets too crowded. On occasion, I've felt as if there were about fifteen entities surrounding me while I was writing their story. Lots of ghosts like their story told, and some actually feel as if they need to let their story be known before they can go where they need to. Hopefully my writing has helped cross over a ghost or two.

Alfred Hitchcock

The legendary, local writer, filmmaker, and producer Alfred Hitchcock was known for his thriller and horror movies, particularly his hit flick, *Psycho,* made in 1960. The Sunshine Villa located on Front Street (see Sunshine Villa story) is what inspired Hitchcock to write the film. The home was the Old McCray Hotel at the time. The place not only looked haunted, it was. The decrepit structure was so eerie and enchanting, that Hitchcock made the Bates mansion in his movie *Psycho* very similar to the haunted hotel, located on Beach Hill in Santa Cruz.

That same year, Hitchcock won an Academy Award for best director, and also received an honorary doctorate for "magnificent accomplishment in the world of cinema," presented by The University of California, Santa Cruz.

In 1950, Hitchcock, his wife, and daughter moved to an exquisite nine-bedroom Spanish mansion on a large mountaintop in Scotts Valley. He was always fascinated with Santa Cruz's historic buildings, and thought it would be a good place to live and write.

In 1961, a strange event took place in Capitola that inspired Hitchcock to write his next famous film *The Birds,* released in 1963. Late in the night on August 21, 1961, huge flocks of seagulls "invaded" the area from Pleasure Point to Rio Del Mar Beach. Hundreds of seabirds fell from the sky and collided into homes. Scientists could not determine why the birds came down is such an odd fashion.

Hitchcock was a local resident of Santa Cruz County until 1974. The creative genius, also known as "the master of suspense," was said to be very serious, but also very funny at times. One of Hitchcock's most famous quotes was, "The length of a film should be directly related to the endurance of the human bladder."

After directing more than fifty films, the eighty-year-old legend died peacefully in his sleep from kidney failure on April 29, 1980, in Bel Air, California. Hitchcock was then cremated, his ashes spread along the Pacific Ocean. His funeral was held in Beverly Hills at the Good Sheppard Catholic Church. Although Hitchcock is no longer with us, his time in Santa Cruz County still echoes with his glory.

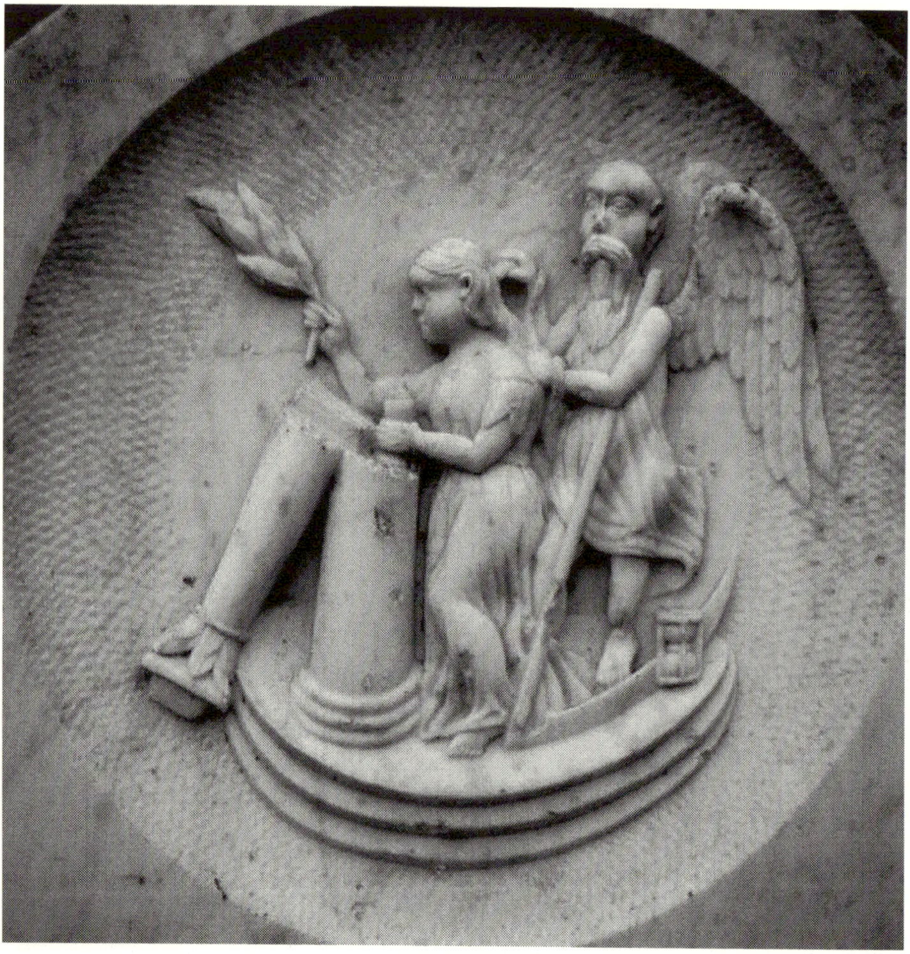

GLOSSARY

Cold Spot: A small, defined area of intense cold that is at least ten degrees colder than the surrounding area, believed to be caused by a ghost when there is no natural or mechanical explanation.

Conduit: A person or an object that attracts or draws in spirits for various reasons.

Dowsing Rods (AKA Divining Rods): Two metal, L-shaped rods that move on their own. The dowsing rods have been used for centuries to find rock, graves, water, and any type of solids underneath the Earth. While standing above an area with solid material below, the rods will cross. Paranormal investigators have been using rods for years to communicate with spirits. The entities are able to move the rods for *Yes* and *No* responses.

Ectoplasm: Spiritual energy that takes form of fluid or mist.

EMF: Electromagnetic field.

EVP (Electronic Voice Phenomenon): A disembodied voice heard through white noise or on a recorder.

Flashlight method: A technique that's used to communicate with spirits by setting a screw-top mini Mag-light on a hard surface and asking the spirit(s) to turn the flashlight on and off on command.

Ghost (Spirit) Box: An electronic device that allows you to listen in between radio frequencies to communicate with spirits through the white noise.

Ghost Radar: An application you can download on most mobile devices that can detect paranormal activity. It measures electromagnetic fields and identifies energies when they are near. The application also has a built-in Ovilus, which provides a large vocabulary list for spirits to choose from. The app then "speaks" the words chosen.

Incubus: An evil male entity who is said to rape individuals, typically in their sleep.

K-2 Meter: A scientific instrument that measures electrometric fields. It is believed that ghosts give off electromagnetic energy which can be picked up on an EMF Detector or K-2 Meter.

Medium: A person who is able to channel and communicate with spirits.

Mel Meter: A device that measures electromagnetic fields and temperature.

Orb: An energy anomaly, normally seen in photographs or on camera, and sometimes witnessed by the naked eye. The circular ball of light has been seen in different colors, and moving in diverse speeds and directions. It is believed to be a spirit in transit.

Pendulum: A weight hung by a fixed support that moves under the influence of gravity. Some ghost hunters use pendulums, most commonly made out of a mineral and hung by a string, so that it's easy for spirits to move and manipulate it.

Photo Psychic: A psychic who is able to *see* images in photographs that are not visible to most. They can also pick up on emotions or information just by looking at a photo.

Sensitive: Psychic

Spirit Guide: A disembodied force that guides you through life. Everyone is said to have at least one spirit guide, and some have up to five, these guides can change throughout a person's life. Most can't feel, hear, or see their guides, but that doesn't mean they don't exist.

Trigger Object: An object that can help trigger ghosts to communicate and/or create activity. Some ghost hunters place an object somewhere in the haunted area that a spirit may be attracted to, such as, leaving a ball or a doll out, for a little girl spirit.

Vortex: A doorway or portal to another realm that allows entities and other paranormal phenomena to come into our world.

More Books by Aubrey Graves

Supernatural Santa Cruz, 2011

Ghosts of Santa Clara County, 2012

The Unofficial Guide to Disneyland's Haunted Kingdom, 2012

The Haunted Brookdale Lodge, 2014

Please visit my website www.aubreygraves.com for details.

Supernatural Santa Cruz - Second Edition
Aubrey Graves

The Santa Cruz Beach Boardwalk, Santa Cruz, CA. Photo by Debi Parola- All rights reserved.

Sources

Books:

- Beal, Chandra Moira, and Beal, Richard. *Santa Cruz Beach Boardwalk: The Early Years - Never a Dull Moment*. U.S.A.: The Pacific Group; 2003.
- Chase, John. *The Sidewalk Companion to Santa Cruz Architecture*. Santa Cruz, CA: Paper Vision Press; 1979.
- Dennett, Preston. *Supernatural California*. Pennsylvania: Schiffer Publishing Ltd.; 2006.
- Dwyer, Jeff. *Ghost Hunter's Guide to Monterey and California's Central Coast*. Gretna, Louisiana: Pelican Publishing Co.; 2010.
- Graves, Aubrey. *Supernatural Santa Cruz*. Charleston, South Carolina: Createspace; 2011.
- Graves, Aubrey. *Paranormal Investigations of Santa Cruz County*. Charleston, South Carolina: Createspace; 2012.
- Graves, Aubrey. *Ghosts of Santa Clara County*. Charleston, South Carolina: Createspace; 2012.
- Guiley, Rosemary Ellen. *The Encyclopedia of Ghosts and Spirits, Second Edition*. New York: Checkmark Books; 1992.
- Koch, Margaret. *The Walk Around Santa Cruz Book*. Fresno, CA: Valley Publishers; 1978.
- May, Antoinette. *Haunted Houses and Wondering Ghosts of California*. San Francisco, CA: The SF examiner division of the hearst corporation; 1977
- Perry, Frank A; Piwarzyk, Robert W; Luther, Michael D; Orlando, Alverda; Molho, Allan; Perry, Sierra L. *Lime Kiln Legacies- The History of the Lime Industry in Santa Cruz County*. Santa Cruz: The Museum of Art and History; 2007.
- Reinstedt, Randall A. *California Ghost Notes*. Carmel, CA: Ghost Town Publications; 2000.

Santa Cruz Sentinel Articles:

- Anonymous Author. "Glamour, gangsters and ghosts: Brookdale Lodge possesses colorful history." 8/19/09
- Anonymous Author. "Haunted Houses of Santa Cruz." 10/31/82
- Baine, Wallace. "A Strange History of a Strange Place." 5/29/09
- Guzman, Isaiah. "Ghostbusters Scour Brookdale Lodge." 1/19/08
- Guzman, Isaiah. "Stirring Up Spirits." 1/11/08
- Issacson, Joel. "Old Holy Cross Cemetery Suffers from Vandalism." 12/28/08
- Koch, Margaret. "Ghost Stories: Bizarre Tales Haunt Local History." 1/22/91

Supernatural Santa Cruz - Second Edition
Aubrey Graves

- Lawshe, Mark. "Ghost Story of Sarah Cowell." 10/30/75
- Lawshe, Mark. "Goblins, Ghosts In the Area." 10/29/75
- Mickelson, Gwen. "Fabled Brookdale Lodge - - Ghost and all - - Up for Sale." 5/17/07
- Morgan, Terri. "A Halloween Tale: The Curse of Pogonip." 10/31/06
- Musitelli, Robin. "Ghostly Goings on at Haunted Houses." 10/27/96
- Parker, Ann. "Spirited Dining at the Brookdale Lodge." 9/14/05
- Parker, Ann. "Spirited goings-on at Scottish Pub." 5/14/06
- Robinson, John. "Ghosts Said to Haunt Hotel." 10/31/86
- Seals, Brian. "La Conchita Mudslide Stirs Memories of Love Creek Catastrophe." 1/13/05
- Swift, Carolyn. "Rispin is a Setting Worthy of the Spirit World." 10/31/99
- Townsend, Peggy. "Ghost Stories: Voices, Ghouls and a Love That Lasts Forever." 10/31/04
- Trabing, Wally. "Old Santa Cruz Ghost Story." 1/30/75
- Tryde, Wendy. "Ghosts of an Old Hotel." 10/31/00
- Walch, Bob. "Brookdale Lodge's Ghost Intrigues Tourists." 10/25/07

Other Articles:

- Allen-Taylor, Douglas. "Tales of Three Ghosts." Metroactive, 1999
- Anonymous. "Psyching Out the Spirits." San Francisco Sunday Examiner & Chronicle, 10/30/77
- Anonymous. "Best Arts and Entertainment." Good Times. 4/25/12
- Asch, Jennifer. "Greetings from Santa Creepy / in and around Santa Cruz, ghost stories and spooky sites send chills up visitors' spines." San Francisco Chronicle, 10/31/97
- Harbert, Gregory Jon. "Old Santa Cruz Haunts." Valley Press/ Scotts Valley Banner, 1999
- Jacobson, Kate. "Ghost Riding in Santa Cruz." Santa Cruz Weekly, 10/28/10
- Martin, Christa. "Visiting Some of Our Favorite Haunts." Good Times, 10/19/00
- Orion, Damon. "Surreal Estate." Good Times, 6/10/99
- Phelan, Sarah. "Hex Appeal." Metro Santa Cruz, 9/6/02
- Phelan, Sarah. "The Ghost Stays in the Picture." Metro Santa Cruz, 10/9/02
- Phelan, Sarah. "The Haunting of Santa Cruz." Metro Santa Cruz, 10/29/03
- Rogers, Paul. "Dislodging the Ghosts? Eerie Events at Hotel Rattle Owners, Lead top Exorcism." Mercury News, 1/4/91
- Spicuzza, Mary. "Santa Cruz Suburban Legends." Metro Santa Cruz. 1999.
- Unknown (Anonymous) "Fact or Fright Fiction." Morgan Hill Times. 10/28/05

Supernatural Santa Cruz - Second Edition
Aubrey Graves

Papers:

- Eng, Julie. "Walking With a Ghost." City on a Hill Press: A student-run newspaper. 2010

Websites:

- http://coursetrained.blogspot.com/2008/08/lost-tunnels-los-gatos-to-santa-cruz.html
- http://darkhaunts.com/CaliforniaGhostStoryIndexPAGE2.html
- http://en.allexperts.com/q/California-89/f/Mount-Madonna.htm
- http://en.wikipedia.org/wiki/Alfred_Hitchcock
- http://en.wikipedia.org/wiki/California_State_Route_17
- http://en.wikipedia.org/wiki/Laurel,_California
- http://en.wikipedia.org/wiki/Patterson-Gimlin_film
- http://en.wikipedia.org/wiki/Talk%3ALimestone#Limestone_in_haunted_locations.3F.3F.3F
- http://ghost-girls.org/
- http://gocalifornia.about.com/od/camissions/ss/mission-santa-cruz_2.htm
- http://kfrc.radio.com/2010/10/25/bay-areas-most-haunted-places/
- http://naturalplane.blogspot.com/2011/04/bobo-enigma-of-monterey-bay.html?utm_source=feedburner&utm_medium=feed&utm_campaign=Feed%3A+PhantomsAndMonstersAPersonalJourney+(Phantoms+and+Monsters)
- http://researchforum.santacruzmah.org/viewtopic.php?t=75&view=next&sid=5c95bf280c0cf5e180547c751854a55f
- http://researchforum.santacruzmah.org/viewtopic.php?t=83
- http://santacruzparanormalresearch.blogspot.com/2009/02/partial-catalog-of-haunted-places-in-sc.html
- http://scplweb.santacruzpl.org/history/spanish/kimholy.shtml
- http://sluggosghoststories.blogspot.com/2009/05/porter-college-university-of-california.html
- http://sluggosghoststories.blogspot.com/2009/06/white-lady-of-graham-hill-road.html
- http://theshadowlands.net
- http://theshadowlands.net/ghost/ghost442.html
- http://www.angelfire.com
- http://www.athanasius.com/camission/cruz.htm
- http://www.bigfootdiscoveryproject.com/
- http://www.capitolamuseum.org/1930rispin.html
- http://www.carpenoctem.tv/haunt/ca/

Supernatural Santa Cruz - Second Edition
Aubrey Graves

- http://www.cityonahillpress.com/2010/11/18/walking-with-a-ghost/
- http://www.cliffcrestinn.com/
- http://www.examiner.com/arizona-haunted-sites-in-phoenix/arizona-ghost-hunter-travels-roaring-camp-railroad-ghost
- http://www.ghostsofamerica.com
- http://www.ghoststudy.com/ghost%20stories/sep00/santacruz.html
- http://www.hauntedbay.com
- http://www.hauntedhouses.com/states/ca/
- http://www.legendsofamerica.com/ca-hauntedhotels3.html
- http://www.liparanormalinvestigators.com/rocks.shtml
- http://www.mcpost.com/article.php?id=773
- http://www.mnn.net/roarhike.htm
- http://www.montereycountyweekly.com/news/2007/oct/25/monster-swell/
- http://www.npr.org/programs/lnfsound/scrapbook/kitchensisters.html
- http://www.nuforc.org/webreports/046/S46523.html
- http://www.redmanhouse.com/history.shtml
- http://www.roaringcamp.com/pdfs/RoaringCampHistory.pdf
- http://www.santacruzpl.org/history/articles/183/
- http://www.santacruzpl.org/history/articles/446/
- http://www.santacruzsentinel.com/ci_15163347
- http://www.scparks.com/highlands.html
- http://www.seabreezetavern.com/history.html
- http://www.shadowbrook-capitola.com/
- http://www.strangeusa.com
- http://www.svchamber.org/svhistory/history/hitchcock.htm
- http://www.thecobrasnose.com/xxghost/santacruz.html
- http://www.unexplainable.net/artman/publish/article_14552.shtml
- http://www.valleyhaunts.net/showthread.php?tid=88
- http://www.vaughns-1-pagers.com/history/rispin-mansion.htm
- http://www.waymarking.com/waymarks/WM59HT_Blue_plaque_Veterans_Memorial_Building_Watsonville_California
- http://www.yourghoststories.com/real-ghost-story.php?story=879
- http://www3.gendisasters.com/california/15542/big-tree-ca-train-wrecked-may-1880?page=0%2C0
- www.charlespeden.wordpress.com

Videos:

- *Bigfoot Discovery Day IV.* "Mike Rugg - Santa Cruz Sasquatch," 2010

Supernatural Santa Cruz - Second Edition
Aubrey Graves

- http://www.dailymotion.com/video/x90bt4_are-mystery-spot-eye-illusions-real_shortfilms
- http://www.facebook.com/video/video.php?v=102519193106148&oid=169750553373&comments
- http://www.seasideparanormal.com/tv-show.htm

Notes

Supernatural Santa Cruz - Second Edition
Aubrey Graves

Supernatural Santa Cruz - Second Edition
Aubrey Graves

About the Author

Paranormal investigator and empath Aubrey Graves has always had a vast interest in the supernatural. She resides in Santa Cruz, California with both the living and the dead.

aubreygraves@hotmail.com

Made in the USA
Middletown, DE
05 September 2023